Ten Secrets of Successful Leaders

Ten Secrets of Successful Leaders

The Strategies, Skills, and Knowledge Leaders at Every Level Need to Succeed

⌇

Dr. Donna Brooks and Dr. Lynn Brooks

McGraw-Hill

New York Chicago San Francisco Lisbon London
Madrid Mexico City Milan New Delhi San Juan
Seoul Singapore Sydney Toronto

The *McGraw·Hill* Companies

1 2 3 4 5 6 7 8 9 0   **DOC/DOC**   0 9 8 7 6 5

ISBN 0-07-145373-3

McGraw-Hill books are available at special quantity discounts to use as premiums and sales promotions, or for use in corporate training programs. For more information, please write to the Director of Special Sales, Professional Publishing, McGraw-Hill, Two Penn Plaza, New York, NY 10121-2298. Or contact your local bookstore.

 This book is printed on recycled, acid-free paper containing a minimum of 50% recycled, de-inked fiber.

Contents

Participants

We would like to extend our appreciation to the following leaders and organizations who shared their views, insights, and passion:

- Marcia J. Avedon, Ph.D., Senior Vice President, Human Resources, Merck & Co., Inc.
- Lynn Badaracco, Director, Emerging Leaders Programs, Sprint
- Frank Bisignano, CEO of Global Transaction Services, Citigroup
- Sally Bonneywell, Director, Executive Development and Talent Management, GlaxoSmithKline
- Lawrence P. Clark, Ph.D., Assistant Vice President, New York Life
- Virginia Clark, Vice President, Unisys University
- Anne Connery-Lee, Director, Leadership & Organizational Development, Janssen Ortho-McNeil, a Division of the Johnson & Johnson Companies
- Frank Cuttita, Managing Director and Chief Administrative Officer, Columbus Circle Investors
- Professor Dame Sandra Dawson, Director of the Judge Institute of Management, University of Cambridge and Master of Sidney Sussex College Cambridge
- David Deacon, Managing Director, Global Head of Executive Development, Credit Suisse First Boston
- Gary Dibb, Ph.D., Chief Administrative Officer, Barclays Bank
- Ben E. Dowell, Ph.D., VP, Talent Management, Bristol-Myers Squibb Company

- Beverly Edgehill, Vice President, Leadership & Learning, Fidelity Investments
- GE Commercial Finance
- General Motors
- Tracy Evans Gkonos
- Rosemarie B. Greco, Director, Pennsylvania Governor's Office of Health Care Reform
- Doug Green, Partner in Charge, Leadership Development, KPMG, LLP
- Dave Groff, Chief Learning Officer, Allstate Insurance Co.
- Stephen Handy, Chief Learning Officer, FedEx
- Ted Hoff, Vice President, Learning, IBM
- Richard M. Jacobs, Ph.D., Associate Professor, Villanova University
- Roberta LaRocca, Associate Director, Headquarters Integration Office, Wyeth Pharmaceuticals
- LaSalle University
- Mona Lau, Group Head of Diversity, UBS
- Luiz Lima, Managing Director, Citigroup
- Michael Maffucci, Director of Leadership Development, Deutschebank AG
- Robert Mann, Member of the Group Managing Board and Global Head of Learning and Development, UBS
- Ray McGowen, Global Vice Chair, Ernst & Young
- Drew Morton, Director, Management Development, IBM
- Ralph W. Muller, Chief Executive Officer, University of Pennsylvania Health System
- Rebecca Nelson, First Vice President, GPC Learning & Development, Merrill Lynch
- Eugene D. O'Kelly, Chairman and Chief Executive Officer, KPMG, LLP
- Tim O'Toole, Managing Director, London Underground, Ltd.
- Rajeev Peshawaria, Executive Director, Head of Pine Street and Learning and Professional Development, Europe, Goldman Sachs & Co.
- Carol Pledger, Managing Director, Global Head of Learning and Professional Development, Goldman Sachs & Co.

- Sandra Price, Vice President, Human Resources, Talent Management, Sprint
- Gill Rider, Chief Leadership Officer, Accenture
- Christopher C. Safsten, Senior Manager, Booz Allen Hamilton
- Ralph W. Shrader, Ph.D., Chairman and Chief Executive Officer, Booz Allen Hamilton
- Coleen A. Smith, VP Global People Development & Staffing, Global Education & Training, Employee Relations/Best Place to Work, Colgate Palmolive
- Temple University
- Allen Thomas, National Managing Partner for Human Resources, Deloitte & Touche USA LLP
- Richard Thorne, Managing Director, Worldwide Business Development, Innovata LLC
- Doug Trainor, Director, Team Leader, Leadership Education and Development, Pfizer, Inc.
- The Vanguard Group
- Yvette Vargas, SVP, Talent/Performance, JPMorganChase

We also would like to express our great appreciation to those participants who have chosen to remain anonymous.

Introduction

The New Epic Leader

౿ఌ

As corporations face the challenges of global competition, their leadership capabilities have become paramount for success. With leadership high on the list of CEO priorities and corporations short on leaders, the selection, development, and deployment of business leaders have become top priorities.[1]

WHO WILL BE INTERESTED IN THIS INFORMATION?

First, anyone interested in leadership—from those aspiring to their first leadership position to senior managers seeking to move to the next level—undoubtedly will find the insights and information from CEOs and other top leaders invaluable. They will learn how experienced leaders build and lead successful, results-oriented teams; are effective in an increasingly complex, uncertain environment of rapid change and a range of threats; and passionately communicate their vision. We asked these leaders several questions, including "What advice would you give to the next generation of leaders?" and "What is your 'wish list' of skills, knowledge, and behaviors for leaders of the future?" Some of their answers may surprise you.

In addition, hiring managers and leaders at all levels will be anxious to hear some of the outstanding insights on the skills, knowledge, and behaviors essential to leaders of the future. Furthermore, we will detail how managers can prepare the next generation of leaders to take their place in the organization while positioning themselves for their own next challenge. We will discuss the major challenges facing organizations today, as well as the advice, solutions, and strategies they have put in place to address these challenges.

Finally, leadership development specialists and experts undoubtedly will appreciate the insights, strategies, and best practices of their peers across industries. They will learn what some of the best companies are doing about globalization, diversity, tying goals to business strategy, measuring the effectiveness of their initiatives, and other critical issues.

These and many other topics surely will be of interest to anyone interested in the challenges of and strategies for effective leadership.

WHAT CAN LEADERS OF THE FUTURE EXPECT?

In our research on leadership, as well as in our discussions with thought leaders worldwide, we have consistently seen evidence of a critical shortage of leaders—and potential leaders—especially on a global level. Many of our clients have commented on their organizations' plight—too many key positions and not enough qualified people to fill them. It harkens somewhat back to the technology-driven glory days of the 1990s—organizations around the world were desperate for the smart, young, talented, and often cocky "techies" who had the skills (and knew it). They held the key to individual and organizational success at that time. Luring these technology demigods with perks and payouts, organizations thought they had exactly what they needed to secure their strategic competitive advantage. Well, we all know what happened to most of them! As a result of the economic downturn at the turn of the century and worldwide uncertainty on many levels, there is now an increased realization that a new set of leadership skills, knowledge, and behaviors is necessary for leadership across organizations. We have seen an evolution both in the research and in our own experiences of another trend—or rather need—emerging for the next generation of leaders.

A recent Conference Board CEO study entitled, "Developing Leaders for 2010,"[2] underscores some of the specific challenges and issues that both nonprofit and for-profit organizations worldwide will confront: globalization, hypercompetition, enormous scientific and social change, rapid advances in technology, and growing diversity among the workforce, customers, and other stakeholders.

In response to the challenges they have identified, the Conference Board also has compiled a preliminary list of specific skills, knowledge, and capabilities that the next generation of leaders will require to succeed in this increasingly complex environment: strategic thinking, particularly with regard to global competition and the application of technology; analytical capability to sort through large amounts of information to focus on the most relevant aspects; the capacity to influence and persuade highly diverse groups of employees, customers, strategic partners, investors, and other stakeholders; the ability to lead in an environment that spans global cultures; and a high level of personal adaptability to learn from experience and adjust course accordingly.

However, just at the time when the need is exploding, the demand for these leaders is far outstripping supply. When talking about the imminent war for talent, one of our interview participants added, "Well, the war has started." Another CEO added, "We have about three years' worth of projects on the table with no one to lead them." So what's the problem—why do they have such a talent crisis?

First, as the McKinsey study, "The War for Talent," indicates, many current leaders are retiring, and demographically, there are simply not enough members of the upcoming generation to replace them. In fact, between 1998 and 2008, the number of 25- to 44-year-olds (those traditionally in the pool for leadership positions) will decrease by 6 percent.[3]

In simple terms, this means that there will be a shortage of managerial talent to effectively lead a company or division or to supervise and motivate a new product team. (And we're not yet even addressing the issues of people who must be able to mobilize and motivate their teams in times of crisis or to respond quickly and effectively to the complex questions that arise minute by minute on the financial trading floor, in the high-tech environment, or on the manufacturing plant assembly line.) In addition, there is not a large enough talent pool with the broad range of skills essential in our rapidly changing environment. There is a human and intellectual capital shortage, a "smart people gap."

Second, and almost more important, everyone is competing for the same people within this shrinking pool who have these coveted skills, knowledge, and behaviors regardless of organization, industry, or global location. Literally everyone on earth is looking for the exact same people—organizations worldwide will have to compete intensely for this limited supply of talented managers for at least the next two decades. Who are these elusive, sought-after superstars? Surpassing the capabilities of traditional white-collar workers or technology gurus of the past, these are the people whom everyone wants *on* their team, *leading* their team—the so-called gold-collar workers.[4] They have complex capabilities—they possess far more than outstanding technical skills. They are able to communicate and persuade, as well as to lead teams with passion, energy, and inclusiveness. They also have a keen self–awareness and, often, surprisingly little ego. With a firm, ethical stance and ingrained personal values, they also display an intriguing sense of curiosity and often are extremely well read and well informed. They have an innate ability to connect seemingly random ideas or even chaos into a cohesive, clear vision that anyone in their constituency can understand and embrace. They possess an enviable ability not only to survive but also to thrive in an environment of ambiguity, complexity, and uncertainty, taking risks and making smart decisions with limited information or guidance.

To those precious few of you young leaders who have many or most of these qualifications—take comfort—everyone wants you! (Although you who are more experienced and who also have these attributes already know this.) However, those of you in the unenviable position of trying to find these people understand the challenge. Highly qualified new talent is somewhat of a rare breed. Even graduates of MBA programs and other prestigious degree holders don't necessarily have all the pieces of this leadership puzzle covered. Granted, they may have outstanding technical skills and some valuable additional traits or skills. But most leaders admit that they are facing a tall order when it comes to finding future leaders with the full menu of attributes they are seeking. Talent has become an essential component of organizational performance and competitive advantage. Firms that understand the value that these exceptionally talented workers bring also understand that they need to do the best job of attracting, developing, and retaining them. Organizations, then, increasingly must ask, "Why would a talented person choose to work here?" High potentials, future leaders, and emerging leaders—whatever you want to call them—are looking for several key things in organizations. While for some of these young people an attractive compensation package is essential, most of them agree that they want to do work that matters. Culture matters to them—the values of the organization and social responsibility. The opportunity to work with outstanding leaders—to be engaged and challenged—also matters. Equally important is the opportunity to be part of a world-class team or a world-class endeavor and to work with leaders in their field. To this list also add flexibility, the ability to advance, recognition, and an opportunity to work together on global projects.

Unfortunately, many organizations are not in touch with the interests and needs of this most sought-after talent. They either misrepresent the actual environment or opportunities available when recruiting these future superstars, or they fail to deliver on the organizational culture or advancement opportunities that these high-level employees expect when they do secure a position. In addition, many companies do not earn high marks on leadership development, perhaps considering existing training programs adequate for reaching their development goals. Or in the case of mentoring opportunities that are assigned pairings of a more senior with a junior individual—if they happen to get along and the relationship works out, great.

If not, so be it. Just because many managers know *what* they have to do to develop leaders doesn't mean that they necessarily know *how* to do it, have the potential to do it, or have the networks to facilitate getting it done.

However, among many of our participating organizations, leadership development encompasses access to senior role models through well-planned mentoring, coaching, and sponsorship opportunities; opportunities for hands-on experience—rotations, stretch assignments, action learning, and real-world projects and assignments; and frequent feedback using such techniques as 360-degree assessments, among others. These represent fundamental changes not only in their leadership development delivery but also in their organizational cultures as well. There is a systematic effort underway to create a learning environment that embraces diverse perspectives and approaches to the leadership development process. It's a sharing of ideas on learning and development that is being driven at the executive level rather than being viewed simply as a human resources (HR) initiative. The result? Leadership development is linked consistently to strategic business issues and organizational goals.

As one of our participants suggested, developing leaders is gradually evolving from an event to an increasingly well-defined process. In other words, there is a difference between leader development and leadership development. For example, organizations are moving increasingly from focusing *only* on mentoring, 360-degree feedback, and so forth (individual interventions) as the solutions to developing greater leadership to developing and enabling an environment in which sharing knowledge, developing relationships, and collaborative problem-solving can be fostered.

It is increasingly vital to invest in human capital—people's experiences and credentials. These are quickly becoming the basis of competitive advantage for any organization. Many organizations are beginning to realize that it is important not simply to tell people what to do but to help them to find their own way, especially when it comes to taking on challenging problems without solutions that are immediately apparent.

Some people say that you can't necessarily teach leadership to people who don't have the natural talent—and maybe this is true. However, anyone can enhance their skills and maximize their potential. People need career experiences that give them a better understanding of themselves—and others to show them the way.

The bottom line: organizations are desperate for well-prepared, skilled leaders. Given this increasingly diverse environment of rapid change, ambiguity, emerging technologies, and globalization, it is more important than ever to provide a roadmap for individuals and organizations to navigate their course. Therefore, this book is designed to provide practical, real-world strategies and solutions to the issues and challenges that leaders and future leaders share today.

THE NEW EPIC LEADER

Leaders focus on the soft stuff. People. Values. Character. Commitment. A cause. All of the stuff that was supposed to be too goo-goo to count in business. Yet, it's the stuff that real leaders take care of first. And forever. That's why leadership is an art, not a science.[5]

In our research, we asked participants—both leaders and leadership development experts—what they look for in the next generation of leaders. We started to hear a lot of the same responses—some expected, but some rather new. In the past, emerging leaders often were identified because of their outstanding skills, knowledge, and competencies, essentially their track record rather than their future potential as leaders. But this time, in addition to the expected responses, we started to hear a lot more about the "intangibles"—such things as curiosity, passion, energy, emotional intelligence, and "people whom others just want to be around, to follow." Add this to their intellectual horsepower and global perspective and you have a clear picture of what the next generation of successful leaders will look like.

When we started to look at the qualities of these new leaders, the words just jumped out—what people want in their next generation leaders is

Emotional intelligence. Energy. Ethics.

Passion. Persuasion.

Intellectual horsepower. Innovation. International perspective.

Curiosity. Calm in crisis, uncertainty, complexity.

EPIC . . .

Interestingly, when you look up the word *epic*, synonyms that come up include *heroic, ambitious, larger than life, classic, impressive, imposing,* and *grand*.

Think Ulysses, Alexander, Julius Caesar, Henry V. However, in next-generation leaders, most organizations want more. Yes, they want high IQ and high EQ (emotional intelligence), as one of our participants mentioned, but they also increasingly want those intangible skills. As one CEO put it, "What is it about that eighth grader on the ball field that you just know he's going to be a leader? [And it's not the kid who's always yelling, trying to stand out and prove himself.] Everyone wants to be on his team. There's just something about him. . . ." Another leader added her insights: "It seems to be a trend, going from looking strictly at competencies to the more intangible: emotional intelligence, the aura, 'myth and legend.'"

In this book we have sought to understand and share some of the thoughts of leaders and emerging leaders in organizations worldwide, from CEO to chief learning officer to hiring managers to emerging leaders themselves. What skills, competencies, knowledge, and behaviors have made them and others successful? What are the challenges and issues in developing leaders—and what are they doing to meet these challenges? If they could have the perfect combination of skills, competencies, knowledge, and behaviors in up and coming leaders, what would that list include?

So what were some of the initial themes that began to emerge when we asked these questions?

- *Winning the "war for talent."* [6] The best workers—everyone wants them. They have high IQ and high EQ, energy, passion, and excitement. These are the individuals everyone wants to work with—and follow. People want to be a part of what they're doing.

- *Going global.* This is a business imperative, a source of new business. In addition, this means boundary-less organizations (technology, telecommuting, virtual environments, remote locations, global, and working across time zones).

- *Defining competitive advantage.* This means smart, talented, creative people—the more global the better—with great relationships along the supply chain. This collective human capital is an organization's competitive advantage. Personal social capital, human capital, and intellectual capital have become an *individual's* competitive advantage.

- *Mentoring—champions for change, sponsorship.* This involves gaining—and giving—visibility and legitimacy, advice and guidance.

- *Managing your talent strategically—succession management, not just succession planning.* This is what you actively do with the talented people once you've decided who they are.

- *Creating an agile workplace.* This includes learning agility, looking at things in a new way, exploring a variety of experiences, and not recreating the same experience 10 times over.

- *Developing and/or enabling the most important skills and knowledge—but also behaviors.* This is creativity, curiosity, cross-functional/interdisciplinary views, understanding the big picture, and being results-oriented.

- *Understanding the importance of knowledge management.* This involves not just technology but also networks and relationships of all kinds.

- *Recognizing the right chemistry that is needed for each team.* This includes the elements, the intangibles, the behavior, and the style that works best for each team.

- *Leveraging resources.* This includes intellectual, human, and social capital (what we know, what we bring, and who we know).

- *Incorporating ethics.* These are our values, what drives us, and who we are as an individual and an organization. Social responsibility is also a part of this.

- *Communicating effectively.* This involves interacting, persuading, and articulating vision, strategies, and goals, as well as leading teams (especially when you're not the boss).

- *Leading in/managing uncertainty.* This includes projecting confidence and calm in crises, building relationships, decision making, and gathering—and managing—information.

This research is about the issues and challenges that people and organizations worldwide are facing. How people across industries and regions, both domestic and global, are discovering ideas and solutions to problems that can be shared and adapted by others. Many of these organizations are giants in their industries. However, excellent ideas also can be gleaned from people in colleges and universities, hospitals, and government agencies. The issues and challenges of finding and developing leaders are found across the board—so too are many solutions. Many of the strategies in this research are not rocket science—so why isn't every organization just doing it? Lack of access, money, time, commitment, and leadership.

For some organizations there is a tremendous strategic commitment from the CEO, including complex, future-focused analyses underscoring the need for dramatic cultural change and strategic initiatives and business imperatives based on internal and external challenges. However, many who are committed to developing leaders agree that it is tough enough to be innovative in creating leadership talent pools even with total backing of senior management. However, as one participant shares, "If that top-level support is not yet there, it is increasingly vital to develop relationships with everyone—especially senior leaders." It's critical to be able to quantify and present to senior management how interventions align with business strategies. It's also crucial to develop/strengthen your formal and informal relationships with team members and colleagues to execute those initiatives. If you don't think in those terms—learn how to. You need to present a powerful, thoughtful, well-documented message.

Yet it's important to realize that leadership development is not simply the responsibility of "leadership development specialists." It is the responsibility of everyone—at every level. The hiring manager should be thinking: "Are there people I can be considering for this strategic position who I normally wouldn't have thought of? Maybe I need to widen the net, consider those who bring a different set of skills than those I've always considered in the past.... I have to reach out and start mentoring people outside of my usual 'list.'" Emerging leaders themselves should also be proactive in seeking out leadership opportunities and building important relationships with executives and colleagues throughout the organization and beyond. We heard many leaders add that "leadership development is no longer an HR initiative; it's the responsibility of leaders themselves to get involved in attracting, identifying, and developing leaders at all levels."

Likewise, some solutions can be done with a relatively small budget, requiring simply an awareness of and a commitment to enable a collaborative environment to foster better communication and information sharing. Any manager can create a positive culture of open communication and sharing. Any manager can create opportunities for communities of practice and develop enhanced networks—knowing and sharing who is doing what to avoid redundancy, forming knowledge networks, and using technology better. They can identify—and develop relationships with—the people at more senior levels who "get it"—those who can move change along and persuade others to get on board. These managers also can get more senior decision makers to realize that they should identify and consider nontraditional candidates for the pipeline when staffing key positions that lead to senior strategic positions in the future. Much of this can be achieved through better communication, and a number of organizations have begun to do this. However, this book hopefully will provide readers with a wide range of strategies germane to their specific issues and needs through best practices and innovative ideas from a number of leaders in diverse organizations across industries and geography.

Ten Secrets of
Successful Leaders

Cross-Functional/ Interdisciplinary Thinking

Having the Knowledge and Using It

∾

We're looking for people with intellectual capability, but they also have to be able to solve problems and make decisions. As you develop, you are constantly learning to deal with increasing levels of complexity. Adaptability is very important, as well as the ability to influence people. New leaders have to take initiative and show that they know what it takes to get things done. They have to think holistically about how what they're doing fits into the business strategy. They should be able to challenge ideas in an effective way, put the pieces together, and motivate others to follow their lead.

As part of our research process, we asked each of our participants to give us their "wish list"—what they look for in an ideal emerging leader. It was a completely open-ended question, and we had expected a good cross section of skills, knowledge, and behaviors. However, we were surprised at the level to which our participants underscored the importance of "soft skills"—those intangible traits that are hard to measure—and even harder to find in leaders and potential leaders. We had known prior to conducting our interviews that this seemed to be an emerging trend, but we hadn't realized how pervasive it was in the "real world" of leaders.

In the past (and we're talking 5 to10 years ago), organizations were looking for technology gurus, finance wizards, and marketing geniuses—experts in their technical fields. Well, it's no surprise that these people are still in great demand—with one little difference. Now they have to be cross-functional, global, problem-solving, risk-tolerant, big-picture thinkers who just happen to have an outstanding technical expertise. Many leaders believe that the best solutions come from a broad range of disciplines. However, some feel that their traditionally trained managers just don't have what it takes to lead in the twenty-first-century environment and that most MBAs or other business degree programs are too heavily based on technical skills. It's not that there is a shortage of ideas in organizations, but what is missing is the ability to apply new thinking, a new frame of reference to practical, strategic priorities, and then to quickly implement it across the organization. As one participant says: "Our industry is full of very bright people who have extraordinary intellectual horsepower, but who are often clueless about what is happening around them and what their impact on others is."

With the incredible changes taking place in the world at such a rapid rate, most leaders don't have the luxury of conducting studies, pondering decisions, and overthinking every situation. Organizations realize that they need to change faster than the competition to gain and maintain competitive advantage. However, in this environment of uncertainty, volatility, rapid technological change, and competition coming from all sides, most leaders are lucky if they can keep their heads above water. There's often no time to prepare, just to act—or react.

Therefore, what CEOs and other leaders want—and need now—are people who are prepared to jump in when and where necessary. They need individuals who are highly experienced in broad skills such as critical thinking and who can communicate, persuade, inspire, and create. They need people who can develop relationships and build teams. These people also will need to respond quickly to a crisis. Our participants are looking for future leaders who have the courage to challenge assumptions and think outside the box. They want people who will take ideas out of their context and ask, "Why does it have to be done this way just because that's the way it's always been done?" They want people who bring a fresh and new perspective. Leaders often must face complex questions that lack any clear solutions. Organizations need people who can make connections between and among seemingly unrelated issues and make a quick—and appropriate—decision. As one of our participants added, "We're not being paid to just make a simple analysis—anyone can do that. People are paying us to come up with good solutions and make complex decisions."

The bottom line? Organizations are desperate for a cadre of well-informed, global leaders who can see the big picture and manage and lead in a complex, uncertain environment while building and maintaining relationships, mentoring others, and sharing their passion and curiosity to motivate and bring out the best in others. Sound like a tall order? Those of you looking for these leaders know just how tall.

Over a recent dinner, our friend, Bill Schmertz, commented that as technology advances, we will use it less and less for solving what now are complex problems. Advancing technologies will make formerly challenging tasks routine, allowing leaders to concentrate on more complex issues: setting vision, creating strategies, making decisions, and so forth. As the environment becomes more complex and uncertain, organizations increasingly will need people who can—*rapidly*—think, learn, apply best practices, and find out where the knowledge is (who has the knowledge they need and leverage it).

Workers at all levels will be faced with a higher order of knowledge work. For example, this could be the people on technology help lines—those who will need greater problem-solving and communication skills to deal with questions that can't be answered quickly or easily. You can tell which organizations place value on the importance of their first-line staff, the customer service people—and the organizations that don't. They can range from a string of clueless people, all of whom give conflicting information, to highly educated professionals who address every problem at length—and then ask if they can help you with anything else. Think competitive advantage—it's about making that positive first impression on your customers that will build and cement the long-term relationship with them. For example, when calling about one of our business retirement accounts with an investment company a couple of years ago, we were really impressed with the young guy who helped us—more than just pleasant and helpful, he really knew his stuff. Then in our research we talked to people at the company and we understood why. The company starts out young college grads—those on the management track—on the front line to help customers. That's your first impression of the company. Knowledge workers are found in many professions—they're lawyers, engineers, architects, consultants, information technology (IT) professionals, and others. Michael Wonacott calls these workers "gold-collar workers"—the ones every organization wants. Their knowledge is dynamic—it's not just about *having* information but rather *using* it. Their solutions and strategies are often based on experience that may cross functions or disciplines. Another aspect of these "gold-collar workers"—they excel at work that's difficult to assess, evaluate, and reward. It's not about producing widgets. As a result, appraisals, performance metrics, and other HR systems must be reviewed to accommodate this new kind of leader.[1]

Knowledge workers often have interdisciplinary knowledge and experience, and they concurrently apply knowledge from more than one area to solve a problem. Not necessarily married to the idea of only one leader at the top, these individuals increasingly work in teams. They concentrate on results, not simply on the process. Oh, and they are generally in great demand—everyone wants them—so organizations have to work at keeping them. They often may combine different kinds of knowledge: business and technology or science, for example; they often have an understanding of history, philosophy (ethics), foreign language/culture, and literature. They often read voraciously about varied topics of interest. They often value entrepreneurship. They may have an excellent ability to create networks—and they know that they can take their knowledge with them. It's their portable competitive advantage.

The former chairman of Fuji Xerox, Yotaro Kobayashi, is the poster child for this type of interdisciplinary leader. He attended the Aspen Institute, whose syllabus included Plato, Aristotle, and the Old Testament. Subsequently studying religion, history, and culture gave him a deeper insight into his own values on global issues and on diversity. He realized that in order to understand your audience of employees, customers, and your community, you must understand their heritage and values. As a result, he made a point to mentor promising young executives on the importance of a broad understanding of many topics that, at first glance, may not seem to have relevance to the business world. Likewise, Roger Enrico, former CEO of PepsiCo, had many discussions with then-CEO, Don Kendall, early in his career. Enrico credits these talks about opera, Soviet politics, and a wide range of other topics with giving him the valuable insights he later needed as a global leader.[2]

COMPETITIVE ADVANTAGE

During our interviews, many of our participants talked about these gold-collar workers—adding that you often don't even know what it is about them that makes them stand out—it's just something about them. Then imagine the impact when a number of these superstars or emerging superstars get together—it becomes collective knowledge. The result is high energy, excitement, passion, and everyone talking—but also listening carefully. The collective outcome of such a gathering is far greater than the parts. The contagious excitement gets everyone around them motivated and ready to get out there and make a difference. Since many of these key performers gain more insights and energy as they work together, it's not necessarily the model of a single leader at the top—they often like to work in teams. It's the cross-functional, interdisciplinary piece that often sparks innovative ideas. As one participant mentioned: "We are competing against organizations that have basically the same products and technology. We're vying for the same market, so the only thing that differentiates us from our competitors is our people—their knowledge and relationships."

Organizations and their leaders will have to be increasingly aware of who is in their potential pool of gold-collar resources, both internally and externally, to meet their strategic needs. However, it's not enough to simply identify potential members of this group. Organizations also will have to identify their collective competencies, knowledge, and behaviors. They will need to determine how to manage this group, to leverage their talents. Bringing this group together is not like forming a team for a particular project in which people come together for a period of time, complete the task, and then move on. Leaders must create the environment for these valued workers to come together and, preferably, assign a champion in the organization to maximize their opportunities, creativity, and innovation. This is an ongoing process—building and nurturing cross-functional relationships rather than completing a one-time task.

One of our friends recently mentioned that he planned to get his senior team together to do a skills audit as part of the strategic plan. Many of the organizations we talked to are doing the same thing to check their bench strength. They want to know who is in the pipeline, who has what skills, and where the gaps are. However, after that conversation, we started to think, "What skills are most organizations taking into account in their audits?" Yes, it's technical skills, experience, previous positions, and so forth. But what about the more intangible skills, the ones that are harder to identify, to measure, and to assess? Are organizations conducting skills audits to check for integrity, curiosity, emotional intelligence, energy, and passion? What about the ability to think differently and critically, or to make connections between seemingly unconnected information and events? Of course, this is difficult to do. But if leaders are telling us that this is what they're looking for in future leaders, organizations will need to implement measures for the often-intangible soft skills—to explore a new assessment method.

In addition to assessing intangible behaviors and characteristics for *individual* leadership development, a skills assessment also may have to be done for collective leadership development to evaluate how groups of emerging leaders will work together. Beyond tools such as the Myers-Briggs, organizations will have to determine if they've gathered the best potential *group* in terms of innovation, creativity, agility, risk tolerance in dealing with ambiguity, and execution. It's not just chance that certain teams work well together—it's the right mix. Leaders need to be more proactive in identifying not only *who* has worked well together on a certain team but also *why*—what was the best combination of skills, behaviors, personalities, and knowledge? Was it the leadership? Was it the cross-functionality? What seemed to be the best combination of people and personality types for innovation, providing client solutions, or dealing with a global crisis? Bringing in a group of individuals from different areas, functions, or even industries often can be more effective when you want to shake up the status quo, solve a complex problem, or maximize innovation.

Likewise, it may be important for leaders to observe the process itself: how individual team members approach the task, who takes on what role, who speaks, and who doesn't—and other group dynamics issues. What does this achieve? Well, many opportunities to stand out as a potential contributor or leader come in more formal leadership development opportunities after key employees have already been identified for development. But what about those who, for whatever reason, have some potential but perhaps have not yet had the opportunity to shine? Even in the selection process for leadership development, how are the intangibles measured or even identified? It's often just assumed that emerging leaders already have these capabilities early in their career.

During an interview, one leader raised the issue of identifying future leaders: "Why do you think that when we select 25 of our most outstanding people as high potentials that 18 to 20 of them turn out to be unbelievable, but 4 or 5 don't quite meet our expectations—there are others who probably would have been better?" Coincidentally, another one of our leaders had added this interesting insight just the day before:

> *If you're looking at the skills that leaders need—and use—throughout their careers, it's like a graph: on one axis technical skills are needed, on the other leadership skills are needed. The higher up you go in an organization, the more you need leadership skills and the less you need technical skills. However, people are more comfortable talking about technical skills, they're more tangible, easier to quantify. Earlier in their careers, the first five to eight years or so, most high potentials are largely responsible for individual performance and probably use their technical skills about 80 percent of the time—their content expertise, the measurable things, their experiences, what they've done, their past performance. However, you can't measure or accurately predict their potential. You can only extrapolate or guess about the other 20 percent—the unknowns, the intangibles. They haven't used these skills or shown these behaviors for the most part yet—their curiosity, their passion, their influence and inspiration, their ability to bring seemingly random concepts together in a big-picture way. They haven't been put into*

positions for the most part in which these skills, competencies, knowledge, and behaviors have been called into play.

But, as they grow into leadership roles, as they are increasingly responsible for others, the percentages are reversed. The higher the leadership position, the more they rely on the soft skills—the "20 percent" that they used earlier in their career now becomes the 80 percent. Leaders use their technical skills less—they have people under them to give them that information. But what they really need at senior leadership positions are the intangibles—the passion, influence, inspiration, confidence, ability to solve complex problems in an uncertain environment. . . . It's probably a good idea to get these high potentials into leadership experiences earlier in their careers to get a better sense of their aptitude for the softer skills.

How does the above-average but not superstar-level person display his or her aptitude for innovation or creativity, passion, or ability to leverage their social capital if they haven't yet been identified? They may not have had the opportunity for stretch assignments or rotations afforded to high potentials. Experienced leaders should increasingly identify the outstanding B players—solid, hard-working, intelligent performers who just may have more potential than their superiors realize. Perhaps groups and teams can do an informal analysis of how people worked together during the project. Look at the dynamics: Who brought what to the table, who emerged as a leader, and how did the group interact? Get feedback. There are excellent people who may be missed in larger settings but who step up and lead in the right setting. And it's never too late—one senior executive shared his experience as a "late bloomer":

I was over 40 years old—an "operations guy" and content to remain so—when my mentor came to the realization that "maybe this guy can do more." He encouraged me to seek out positions in other functions and in other geographic regions. As a result, I rose to a level in the organization that was far beyond anything I would have imagined possible.

IDENTIFYING THE TALENT— WHO IS GOING TO EMERGE?

No matter how much the research talks about developing leaders at every level, there is sometimes the assumption made that only top management can provide thoughtful insights or generate great new ideas. Emerging leaders sometimes think, well, it's so obvious— someone must have thought of this before. But often they haven't! Innovation and great ideas often come from the most unlikely sources. Leaders should be aware of which names keep coming up with regard to fresh new ideas, innovative approaches, and outside the box thinking. They should listen especially carefully to their informal networks about who is connecting the dots, seeing the big picture, and "getting it." A number of our participants brought up this point. They want future leaders who can see opportunities that have not been considered. They want curious thinkers who are aware of what's going on internally and externally—what's the buzz and what are the trends.

However, one of our leaders added his thoughts on identifying certain traits and skills in potential future leaders:

> *Many of those who are truly exceptional at that age could tend to show what more senior leaders would consider bizarre behavior: too blue sky, too creative, too passionate. But these are exactly the skills that truly outstanding CEOs have—and need—to align strategy, lead people. These young people have a million ideas; they're often smart, creative, disorganized. They don't yet fit the "model" for CEO but have to go through growth and development. They need the right experiences, mentoring, coaching. These days you have two moving targets: a rapidly changing environment and evolving needs for leadership skills, knowledge, competencies. It's tough to find the right people for the future.*

However, in addition to "understanding the big picture" or having a "blue-sky approach," these future leaders also must understand the specific organizational vision and their role within it to see and respond to needs and to come up with strategies and solutions. Leaders are looking to develop talent that has broad-based experience, in addition to specific technical skills. When a future leader makes the transition from individual performer to a leader of others and then to leading a functional team and beyond, new skills have to be developed at each point. A number of our participants talked about their experiences and challenges when they made the transition to managing a function. One finance director was promoted to vice president of technology and finance. Another finance guy took a senior leadership position that encompassed finance, information technology (IT), and even human resources (HR). They had to come to the realization that they were no longer the experts in all the areas for which they now had responsibility. In addition to trusting others for their expertise in various technical areas, they also needed to gain a broader knowledge across disciplines to make key decisions. Further up the leadership line, as a business unit manager or global country manager, leaders essentially become the equivalent of a chief executive officer (CEO) in their area. However, some leaders mentioned the difficulty in transitioning to this level owing to a lack of exposure to and experience in a broad range of functions. A number of our participants agreed that it is extremely important for future leaders to seek out broad-based cross-functional experience early on in their careers. It is especially important for these individuals to seek out lateral positions or long-term assignments in areas outside their technical or functional areas or to get experience in different parts of the business. In addition to doing rotations across functions, they may want to ask for global assignments, preferably ones in which they relocate, not just work as an "expat" or frequent flyer. One of our very senior participants even mentioned that she has to develop a broader nonbusiness background because most of her clients are board-level executives who talk informally about history, the latest books they have read, and so forth. She recognizes the need to go beyond business conversations if she wants to connect with them on a higher level.

Most leaders agree that effective leadership at this level requires more overall knowledge—not necessarily an expertise but at least enough familiarity to be able to ask the right questions of people or to see if something doesn't look right. Leaders increasingly need depth and breadth, as well as a focused expertise. They should be able to challenge long-held assumptions, make decisions based on a logical process, and be able to consider ethics and values in everything they do. Many leaders are derailed at a certain point in their careers by going unprepared into a position in a new part of the business. They may have the technical skills needed but are lacking some of the intangibles. CEOs and leaders at all levels need to make decisions based on limited information and to operate in a rapidly changing, ambiguous, and often volatile environment. To show the way in this new environment, the strongest leaders possess an effective combination of these tangible and intangible skills and behaviors—not an easy thing to find.

THE ART OF LEARNING

A number of our participants talked about what they were looking for in leaders and future leaders—it is the ability to learn. Throughout this book we have been talking about leading in an ambiguous, uncertain, and volatile environment; the importance of thinking critically; and thinking about innovations or solutions that have never been considered. This kind of thinking is sought after and enabled in a learning organization, a learning culture. Not every organization has the luxury of leadership that thinks along these lines—some leaders are still caught up in the idea that there is just one way of doing things—don't ask questions, but just bring us results. But the problem is that most smart young people (the ones every organization wants) don't work this way. They don't care as much about the process, just how to find the solution. A learning organization allows this freedom of thinking and usually gets a better result in return. One leader adds that it's good to allow young leaders to learn from their own mistakes rather than putting too many constraints on them from the outset: "In my opinion, it's better to let people learn from their mistakes. It's better to help guide them [and] then let them live with the impact of their mistakes. Although you should give them some guidance, it's a learning experience to let them dig themselves out."

Another leader talked about what he does to get a sense of his team members' learning styles. "Learning is essential—it's in everything we do. But, it's hard to measure, to get a sense of how people learn. We use one tool—it's a paper and pencil, 360 [-degree] format. It allows us to assess how well a potential leader can learn. The results can range from 'clearly high-potential' to 'solid citizens, good hard workers,' for example. However, interestingly enough, some of these emerging leaders didn't test as well with regard to learning. They can't get over the politics. So, in addition to our formal testing, when we interview candidates, I'll often just talk to them. I ask them about past examples of how they can learn, nonthreatening things. In addition to an interview, I get information from their mentors and sponsors, their bosses. For example, I may ask them if they have ever led, or been involved with, a turnaround, or a startup. What sort of experiences have they had, and what did they learn from them? We have a lot of quantitative people around here—sometimes they're like bulls in a china shop—not necessarily a lot of EQ. However, when they talk about their best people, they say things like, 'I gave someone a number of challenges, and they overcame them and went on to bigger challenges.' They don't necessarily say 'these people are good learners,' but in reality, that's what they are." Another leader adds her thoughts:

> *In the War for Talent, many protégés seem to think that in mentoring relationships the focus is about "me"—I'm important. But mentoring should be a learning tool, [and] sharing wisdom should be about the art of learning.*

WANTED: "ENGINEER WITH MBA WHO READS PLATO"

A number of leaders in our research catalogued the skills, knowledge, and behaviors in their "wish lists" for next-generation leaders. They are looking for future leaders who are inquisitive and curious. They want people with a tolerance for ambiguity and uncertainty, who can analyze and think through a problem, and who see issues in a variety of contexts. They want courageous individuals who can make connections across functions or disciplines and who will challenge assumptions and will stand on a difficult issue. In addition, it is essential that they be able to communicate effectively—to articulate their thoughts and ideas and to persuade others to their rationale. Unlike problem solving, which is generally a step-by-step process that assumes a limited number of possible solutions, critical thinking is more open-ended, reasoning with the possibility of many solutions. It is how insightful individuals approach challenges, problems, and questions. Specifically, asking such things as, "Is there a better way of doing things?" Challenging outdated attitudes or processes. Leaders must be able to raise fundamental questions and formulate them clearly and precisely.

They also must be able to analyze their own value system, as well as the values of others. The most effective leaders are open-minded about divergent views and flexible in taking various opinions into account. They respect others' perspectives and enable an environment in which others can express their true views. They have a tolerance for ambiguity and are able to focus on and approach complex problems from various perspectives. They can create order from chaos. Combining creativity and breadth of thought, these leaders make connections and draw well-considered conclusions. Communication is essential: these leaders have great skill at organizing information well and communicating clearly, concisely, and persuasively. Well prepared for any argument, these leaders are ready for questions and can offer well-thought-out solutions to complex problems. This ability to analyze complex information and come to an appropriate decision based on a logical approach is highly sought after in future leaders. They seek out the best solution or answer, not necessarily the one you want to hear. They are persistent. They benefit from an inquisitive nature—curiosity and an eagerness to learn—even when that knowledge is not readily apparent. These leaders are often well read and work hard at staying well informed. For example, the average CEO reads four to five periodicals and newspapers a day. Successful leaders have a natural curiosity about a wide range of topics. Part of leading is having the confidence both to make the tough decisions without complete information and to change direction if the environment dictates that need—making sound, logical, valid arguments to back up decisions.

Why is it that some individuals have these traits, whereas many others do not? Maybe it's luck, but much of it is experience. Can these traits be learned? Many of our leaders agreed that yes, they have worked at broadening their horizons. Many of them have diverse interests and are voracious readers of history, philosophy, theology, literature, and poetry. They learn other languages. They join colleagues for discussions and debates—academics, scientists, and thought leaders inside and outside their fields. These activities provide a different frame of reference and help to develop higher-order thinking skills, analysis, and synthesis.

One such interesting opportunity is the Educational Leadership Program, now located on Yale's campus. A retreat for leaders at colleges and universities, it offers, among other topics, a reimmersion into liberal arts—an opportunity for intellectual renewal. The program includes a wide range of topics from discussing Plato to reading poetry, from the founders of modern educational thought to the Founding Fathers of democracy. It creates the opportunity for discovery and the ability to think deeply rather than moving quickly from crisis to crisis. Instead of the next golf outing or Outward Bound program, perhaps organizations should consider such a reimmersion in the liberal arts—helping their leaders learn to open their minds, contemplate other solutions, and gain a new perspective.[3]

In this rapidly changing, uncertain environment, not even the most insightful futurist can accurately predict what our world will look like in 10 years. Some of our participants even added that it's almost not worth doing a long-range strategic plan because it will be obsolete in five years. What organizations increasingly need are people who not only can respond to the uncertainties ahead but also are prepared to meet future challenges head on with more creative approaches and a broader perspective.

CHAPTER SUMMARY

Success Secret #1: Cross-Functional/Interdisciplinary Thinking

♦ In order to change faster than the competition in this highly uncertain environment, organizations must identify a cadre of leaders and future leaders who are cross-functional, global, problem-solving, risk-tolerant, big-picture thinkers with outstanding technical expertise—the so-called gold-collar workers. These people make up an organization's competitive advantage. Workers at all levels in a wide range of fields will deal with greater knowledge work: technology help lines, consultants, lawyers, doctors, educators, IT professionals, engineers, architects, and others.

♦ To develop personal competitive advantage, individuals may need to focus increasingly on developing intangible, nontechnical skills and knowledge, in addition to their technical skills. Knowledge workers rely on interdisciplinary knowledge and expertise, often calling on science, mathematics, and logic, as well as history, philosophy, literature, and foreign languages, among many others.

♦ Organizations must understand how to handle these workers—blue-sky thinkers. They often prefer teams, question how things may be done differently, challenge outdated attitudes and processes, focus on results, and are open-minded to divergent views.

Maximizing Your Leadership Style

Leading with Passion, Energy, and Emotional Intelligence

In simplest terms, we look for brains and heart in our leaders. Brains—in terms of intellect and judgment—consist of the wisdom to know what to change and what not to change and the commitment and capability to be the best. Heart—in terms of passion—is the spark that inspires creative solutions, the moral compass to do the right thing, and the personal leadership and interpersonal qualities that can bring others along to make change happen.

If there is one aspect of the new EPIC leader that has emerged in our research, it is that of leadership style—how leaders treat people, their energy, their passion for what they believe in, their ability to inspire others to follow them willingly. They listen; they persuade. They limit their egos—and this doesn't mean hiding their confidence. *Au contraire*, it is understanding that they are one *part* of the leadership process—albeit a critical part. They may have a quiet strength or an extroverted sense of self, but there is a humility about them. After interviewing one chief executive officer (CEO) who was particularly outstanding, we shared our observations of him in our thank-you note. He embodied the definition of a passionate, committed, inspirational leader, and we told him that he reminded us of the "Great One," hockey legend Wayne Gretzky. Every time Gretzky was interviewed following a game, the interviewer invariably would want to hear his blow-by-blow account of the victory—how Gretzky won the game. And invariably Gretzky would respond with something like, "Well, my teammates did a phenomenal job at. . . ." Of course, Gretzky was the reason that the team won, but he never took credit, always recognizing the strength of his team. That's a new EPIC leader. The dean of a major business school adds this interesting insight into this type of leadership:

You can't motivate by numbers alone. You need to give examples of people, their ability to overcome adversity and lead in the face of risk and uncertainty. Yes, you need analysis, but you need to describe your vision in vivid detail with stories.

Over the past several years, as we have conducted research and talked to countless leaders across industries and borders, we have begun to gain a better sense of this attribute. However, it's tough to describe and even harder to measure. When we asked the participants in our interviews to give us a sense of what it is about their emerging leaders, their next-generation leaders, that makes them stand out, the responses were almost unanimous. They agreed that it was something intangible—it's a curiosity, a confidence in the way they present themselves, the way they speak—one leader called it a "boardroom presence." They have a healthy sense of who they are. They're passionate about what they're doing, and they care about their team. Several leaders shared their thoughts:

The greatest distinguisher of leadership is passion and caring— about yourself, your people, your customers, your company. And it must come from the heart; it's not something that's learned. People are sophisticated enough to know if you're sincere—staff, shareholders, media. Who's real and who's giving you a line of B.S. Be honest, available, lay it on the line. People need to really get the sense that you care.

∽

There are different skills that you use at different times in your career, but I have found that a sense of passion and excitement is something that is consistent. It even goes back to something my mother used to say, "If you're not having fun, go do something else." It still holds true today—and it's infectious to the people who work with you. If you walk around with a spring in your step, excited, others can't help but feel that passion and excitement, as well.

Surprisingly, we probably have heard the most about the importance of this type of leadership from military people, former Marines, generals, admirals, and other "tough guys." To a person, they focused on caring for their team, looking out for their people. This was particularly surprising because we had assumed, as probably most other people have, that the military was a "by the book" authoritarian command and control environment. Interestingly, although in some research people have stated that the current leadership model comes from the military command and control—and that we need to change that model—our own experience with military leaders (and those who have crossed over into civilian leadership roles) has been very different. One of our (nonmilitary) corporate leaders even mentioned during our recent interview that "maybe we should start looking at the military model of leading—inspiration, communication, commitment." Our brother, Dr. Victor Brooks, is a military historian, and we frequently share our thoughts on leadership, past and present. One thing that has come up in our discussions time after time is that same idea of looking out for your team, caring for your team. It's fascinating to see the recurring themes throughout history—truly great leadership hasn't really changed that much.

So many of the things that great leaders do are relatively easy to implement by anyone in a leadership role. They get to know their people, and they let their people know they care. They listen, they empathize, and they encourage and support different opinions. All it requires is perhaps a change in personal attitudes and thinking (well, for some people, that isn't so easy). What is considered an "acceptable leadership style" is slowly starting to change. Ten or 20 years ago, no one really cared—or at least did anything—about leaders who led tyrannically, cared only about profits rather than people, but delivered great shareholder value—the "Chainsaw" Al Dunlaps of the world (the title of his book, *Mean Business*, pretty much says it all). But today they are doing something. Given the enormous shortage of talent coming through the pipeline (who can easily go elsewhere), a marketplace that values integrity and social responsibility, and increasingly diverse organizations, leaders are being held more accountable for how they lead. Several of our participants stated that "tough decisions are being made" with regard to leaders who produce great results but have poor attitudes.

There's a lot of talk—justifiably—about the need to change culture. But changing culture is not some event in the abstract—it's organic. It rests on the leadership, changing the perspectives of the organization's leaders. Of course, it can be a huge undertaking, requiring time and often significant cost. In reality, though, it starts with a few people at the top "getting it."

One senior leader put it well when he was describing his organization's enormous culture change. We had been chatting about the fact that it's about individuals recalibrating and reevaluating their perceptions, finding that "a-ha," seeing the light—beginning the change toward a culture that embraces innovation, passion, and empathy that can start with easily doable actions. He shared one of his suggestions: "Publicly compliment your people, not only about things they've done, but how they managed them, how they carried themselves. It's the little things—like saying in front of others—'I really liked the way you handled yourself in that meeting with the CFO. He was tough, and you presented yourself with great confidence and presence. You dealt well with the tough questions.'"

One term that we have been hearing more often is *authentic*. Leaders today need to show people that they care about them, that they're real. People can tell when they're not. One of our participants said of his own role model: "My old boss was a tough task-master, but anyone who ever worked for him agreed—we were all willing to fall on our swords for him. Why? I don't know, he always expected the most from you, but you always wanted to work really hard to make him proud. You always knew that he truly cared about you and recognized your hard work." Another leader, a general who became a corporate leader, shared his thoughts on leading with passion: "The qualities that have served me best in developing my leadership style have been my ability to communicate and motivate. Absolutely critical as well is being genuinely enthusiastic and upbeat, no matter what. Showing the side that's tired, distracted or not engaged gives a sense that you're 'one of the boys,' not what employees want to see in a leader. I believe that people want their leaders to be out in front, showing the way." Other leaders echo his sentiments:

Every once in a while a leader comes in and you don't know what it is, but there's just something about them. You have a sense that something exciting is about to happen and you want to be a part of it.

༚

Leaders should be confident in their self-knowledge—their values, what's important to them. When you get a reputation for results, people want to work with you. You're viewed as a change agent who energizes others around that change. You see goals, not obstacles— you don't get waylaid.

༚

If you show people that you appreciate them, it energizes them. Sometimes it can be just an e-mail or thank-you note. They want to perform for you, they want to exceed their limits of what you think they can do.

DEVELOP YOUR PEOPLE, CARE FOR YOUR TEAM

A major theme that emerged in our research was the importance of developing your people—a number of our leaders felt very strongly about this. Whereas in the past people were assessed and rewarded on their individual merits, increasingly they are responsible for bringing others along as part of their role. Likewise, General Electric (GE) CEO Jeffrey Immelt, like his predecessor Jack Welch, spends a lot of time building personal networks worldwide, connecting with people across the company. He adds, "When I meet someone, I look for the person with the great instinctive feel for his market, his business, and his subordinates. When I do a Session C, half the grade I give is to the individuals and half is to their team. I ask 'Who's in your wallet?' I want to see who's in their family, who they brought with them in their careers. Some people's wallets have no pictures. Some can pull out a whole family album. That is extremely important."[1]

Another consistent message we heard from our leaders was the importance of letting people know that they are cared about and having your actions reflect your words. Leaders often show their true colors in a crisis. For example, one New York CEO illustrated this leadership quality following the World Trade Center attack. He greeted employees in the lobby when they returned to work. It wasn't anything formal, just a "Welcome back" and "How are you? Are you okay?" Yet it generated an unbelievable response among his employees. During times of crisis, showing emotion is okay—it's welcome. People also want their leaders to be confident—to assure them that everything will be all right.

LEADERSHIP AND EGO

One of the comments that we have been hearing much more frequently focuses on the importance of ego and gaining a sense of who you are. As one leader stated: "As you hire people, get the best you can find—the smartest, the most capable. Some people can be uncomfortable or intimidated with this approach, but in reality, the best people will only make you look better." This strategy worked especially well for John F. Kennedy and Ronald Reagan, for example. Kennedy, highly intellectual himself, gathered a number of academics and others who had been spurned by previous administrations to serve in his own cabinet. Likewise, Reagan made no bones about saying that he prided himself on surrounding himself with people who were smarter than he. We heard this same sentiment expressed a number of times by our participants. Actually, we know a lot of people who follow this strategy successfully, and they're some of the brightest, most talented, and successful people we know. However, one thing that connects them all is an overriding comfort with who they are. They don't need to pull rank or demand respect—they have earned it through their actions, their accomplishments, and their intelligence. As one CEO said, "Today's leaders need to show humility. No one can be an expert at everything, and they need to rely on the expertise of others." Another leader concurs: "Use your own special strengths. If you can't engage people, you won't get the best from them. At the end of the day, they must trust you, believe in you, and respect you in order to cause change. And this is built over years, not days. It takes time. You have to cause people to want to follow you." Many people are starting to recognize this trait as emotional intelligence, or EQ.

EMOTIONAL INTELLIGENCE

Using Daniel Goleman's concept of emotional intelligence[2] as a foundation, many leaders we spoke with expressed their own interpretations of this theme. So what do they see as the critical elements? More than just keeping one's emotions in check, it's to do with a general self-awareness, ego, and making decisions with others' interests in mind. It's humility when you need it, but confidence as well. It's positive thinking and resilience— finding solutions to setbacks and inspiring others to believe. It's the ability to communicate—to listen to others and empathize with their emotion, their perspectives, and their challenges. It is to inspire and persuade rather than dictate and to lead with passion and energy. It involves effectively dealing with emotions such as fear and anger and coping with challenges. It means working effectively with others and understanding the importance of teamwork—not always team leadership. It's *not* being the tough, ego-driven, controlling leader of years past.

Keeping in mind that the workplace is changing, that smart, talented people want leaders who can inspire them, empathize with them, and lead them with passion and energy, managers increasingly will have to address their needs—and possibly adjust their own leadership behaviors accordingly. These overachievers just won't put up with arrogant, egotistical individuals anymore—they can go elsewhere.

However, most people are still not all that comfortable talking about their emotional side—or, in fact, even letting it show. One of our participants talked about a leader program that addressed this issue with outstanding results: "We did a six-week program with some of our leaders, a couple of levels below the senior team. Among other things, we did a 360-degree assessment. Some of the responses included things like 'not sharing credit,' 'not visionary.' However, you realize that 9 out of 10 people don't mean to be jerks—they just aren't aware that there's a problem. It transcends work (their families would probably have told you that they act the same way at home). However, within two weeks of starting the program the changes were incredible, especially in terms of their self-awareness. They changed as leaders, but also as people. It takes a while for the transformation to occur. Now there's a trend toward more collaboration, more teaming. It's trickling down—new 'myths and legends' are being developed." Strong role models are essential in demonstrating this behavior—the influential leader with the ability to show emotion. Several senior leaders shared their insights into this behavior:

The development of Emotional Intelligence in today's environment is the divider between leaders and other people. While it's still very important to develop "technical" skills—things like how to increase market share, problem solving, communication skills, and other general competencies—more important is the ability to develop self-awareness and self-management. Be conscious of the impact that you have on your organization. Coming to this realization early in your career allows you to gain feedback and insights, and to learn from your mistakes. Be able to limit your ego.

ᐁ

Really powerful leaders probably agree that decisions aren't made on their egos—the "Fortune 10" list of leaders are grounded as people; they believe in what they're doing. You can't work on being believable.

CHAPTER SUMMARY
Success Secret #2: Maximizing Your Leadership Style

♦ Great leaders get to know their people; they let their people know they care. They listen. They persuade. They limit their ego. They empathize, and they encourage and support different opinions. Although they expect a lot from their people, great leaders publicly compliment their people and show appreciation for their hard work—they are authentic.

- Increasingly, there are changes in organizational culture that embrace innovation and passion. Great leaders show passion and energy, the sense that "something exciting is about to happen."

- Great leaders have emotional intelligence—they are self-aware and grounded, they learn from their mistakes, and they take feedback as well as give it.

- Talented next-generation leaders want these kinds of leaders—if they can't find them in their current organization, they will move on.

Managing Your Knowledge Networks

✧

As we become a more knowledge-based organization, we expect our people to take on a more independent, semi-autonomous role. We emphasize the fundamental skills that will be sustainable throughout one's career, but there should be a constant building and exchange of knowledge.

Today's economy is the knowledge economy. Ironically, it can be both the problem and the solution. The problem is that the development of a knowledge economy now demands rapid knowledge sharing—and 24/7 availability—for customers, colleagues, and everyone in the supply chain. However, as a solution, it *facilitates* rapid problem solving, makes better access to information possible, and allows people to be more productive as a result of technological advancements. This speed in sharing knowledge enables employees to get information to their colleagues who need it when they need it. It allows customers to get answers to their questions quickly. It facilitates "just in time" information and solutions to be provided internally and externally across borders, functions, and industries.

With this environment in mind, when we asked our leaders to identify some of the key challenges they face, several themes emerged. One of the major themes was innovation—fostering creativity and creating value, developing a culture of continuous learning, and gaining that important competitive advantage. But how do you enable these intangible behaviors, and how do they become ingrained into the fabric of the organization? For one thing, organizations need to rethink the models of the past, how business is done. Earlier knowledge management models focused essentially on technology—databases (often extremely expensive to develop) and access to reams of information. It was up to the individual to sort it out. Not surprisingly, many organizations realized that this information was largely unused—it brought on information overload—people didn't even know what was available, let alone how to apply it. As the whole concept of knowledge management has evolved, it has begun to encompass far more than just technology. The strategic emphasis now is on not only the knowledge itself but also how to maximize it, share it, and leverage it through human capital. The knowledge, skills, and competencies that are essential for leadership are combined with the development of relationships—creating networks. One leader shares his thoughts on knowledge management:

> *When I think about successful people, they are super intellects with great lateral leadership skills, relationship skills, influence skills. They have the intellectual horsepower to get recognized, but intellect will only go so far—building relationships takes them from there. We have built a culture around bringing people together, forging relationships. Our senior leadership has made this a cornerstone of our business—there are clear accountabilities in place. It is amazing the success we have had in just one year as a result.*

However, this concept is a paradox for many. For years, people have been largely possessive about their knowledge—"If no one else knows what I know, they can't fire me." Yes, individual competitive advantage is what you know, but it is increasingly how you use it—how you add value to the organization. Knowledge now means innovation, creativity, continuous learning, sharing, and collaborating. It's about enabling an environment in which these networks can develop, grow, and evolve. It involves creative thinking—actually *using* what you know, not just knowing it. It encompasses your human capital (your experiences) and intellectual capital (*what* your know) but also social capital (*who* you know): employees, customers, partners, and your supply chain. Future corporate performance will be tied closely to human capital—*what* individuals bring to the organization in addition to *who* they know—their human relationships.

Innovation, knowledge, and creativity—essential elements of corporate performance and advantage in the marketplace—often stem from smart, creative individuals working together: sharing information and new ideas, finding support and encouragement from colleagues and team members, and taking an idea and envisioning numerous applications for it. Innovation has the ability to grow exponentially in a supportive learning environment.

DEVELOPING COMPETITIVE ADVANTAGE

Many leaders will agree that the most important product, the major value of most organizations today, comes from their knowledge. In a recent chief executive officer (CEO) survey, 60 percent of the participants noted that knowledge management is critical to company success.[1] We work with many professional services companies, including financial and consulting firms, for whom knowledge is their only product. And in many cases their product is not protected from competitors. Their clients expect them to deliver results. Their intellectual capital, innovative solutions, and ability to leverage their knowledge are key to creating sustained growth and competitive advantage. As one leader says: "It's all about ideas. Intellectual property is unprotected. High-margin products can quickly become commodities. Your people have to be constantly generating new ideas." In order to harness and maximize this enormous collective knowledge and apply it to real-world challenges, you need people at the top who can make these connections, see the big picture, and think outside the box to get the right mix of people together. Leaders must understand their environment, their workers, and their customers more effectively. They need to assess, challenge, and reevaluate assumptions about their strategic direction. Knowledge rather than product or market position is the number one competitive advantage an organization has. With this in mind, leaders increasingly need to adjust (or completely change) how they view their culture, their systems, and their relationships—how knowledge flows, how they lead, and how to maximize individual and team performance.

Individual competitive advantage is dynamic—people become well known and well regarded through their ability to keep coming up with new applications for their knowledge, new ways of thinking, and new ways to maximize and leverage their knowledge. But those people don't work in a vacuum. We have spoken to many of them—they join or start formal or informal think tanks, and they surround themselves with thought leaders—people with the same enthusiasm and drive. They work on developing effective networks, both internally and externally. As one CEO says: "We work at long-term relationships with our clients—we want to marry our clients, not just date them."

It is essential for leaders to discover who is involved and influential in these networks. They must enable a positive environment for them to flourish and design appropriate incentives for participation, creating the infrastructure to allow the sharing of ideas and information. To develop the kind of environment that enables a free flow of knowledge often requires large-scale cultural change—especially in profitable organizations. What's the incentive to change if the current culture seems to be effective, at least financially? Leaders need to assess the prevailing attitudes and behaviors in their organizations. Do they support a knowledge-sharing culture, or is there a sense of "possession" among teams and functions—"This is *my* info, *my* team, *my* project?" What are leaders doing with people who don't fit a new model despite their performance? What if great performers don't necessarily have great attitudes—arrogance, ego, not willing to help others, to develop others—are the tough decisions being made? How are (human) resources being shared, leveraged, and maximized? Who are the people who get it? Are they in a position to affect change? If not, can they influence those who are?

Creating the concept of a knowledge culture also may require new systems, such as building the ability to include knowledge sharing into performance assessments or determining how teams are put together. Trust and integrity also must be part of the culture—how will these be assessed? One of our leaders commented: "We need to know if are we asking the right questions in the assessment—are they valid for where we want to be going as an organization?"

Several of our participants also talked about the difficulty in measuring success in developing knowledge networks. As one leader said:

> *Our reward systems are generally not set up to recognize group performance and results—we're focused on individual performance. It seems to be easier to recognize the measurable effect a leader has on 600 people in his division than on the 3 or 4 in his network. In addition, I don't know if we are set up to measure intangibles like behavior. We have tried a couple of instruments, but so far nothing has been able to capture and measure what we have wanted it to. It is a challenge to develop a new system of evaluation that fits in this environment.*

Part of the strategic process should focus on how to change the culture so that sharing knowledge rather than keeping it to oneself is rewarded. Many leaders still think of their people in proprietary terms—"my people, my team." As one participant noted: "People aren't anxious to give up their best people. They'll probably never get them back." It's tough to change this culture.

In addition to addressing organizational changes, leaders themselves also may need to change. Leaders need to be role models, embracing and reinforcing changes in attitudes and behavior. A number of our participants underscored the importance of commitment from senior leadership—without the word from the top, a change in culture is not going to happen. What if you don't have the commitment? Then you should start with the leaders and other influential people "who get it." It's surprising how many very smart, well-informed people fail to see and use this informal network of subtle change agents.

What many senior leaders may not consider is that by enabling a knowledge-sharing environment and making a commitment to its implementation, many of the challenges facing them may be addressed more strategically. Knowledge sharing increasingly can foster innovation and creativity, flexibility, and responsiveness. It can enhance cross-functional team effectiveness and allow organizations to locate and share knowledge quickly to respond to environmental changes.

Several of our participants mentioned the importance of developing and maintaining relationships with those above, below, and at one's level. They add that it is important to gain information, knowledge, and diverse perspectives from many sources. As one senior executive adds: "Just because you're a leader doesn't mean that you know everything. There are always more junior people who are better than you. You can learn something from them." One leader makes it a point to get people from across the corporation together, especially young, emerging leaders, and sets up scheduled situations in which they can meet and exchange ideas informally. As a result, there is increased productivity—less reinventing of the wheel on tasks and projects. It's about discovering and leveraging human and other resources and identifying future talent. In addition, a number of our participants have found it very interesting and informative to broaden their perspectives by getting together with thought leaders, academics, and others outside their realm. Others have created domestic or global summits, gathering smart, insightful people from a wide range of industries or disciplines to discuss their common challenges, as well as sharing their best practices and real-world solutions.

CREATING INFORMAL NETWORKS

People admit that they don't often know what's going on elsewhere in the organization. Likewise, they are frequently unaware that others may need the information they possess. It's a gap in the knowledge chain. Individuals may have outstanding skills and experiences not directly connected with their current position that could greatly enhance a new team or project—but again, no one knows about them, and the individual doesn't realize that he could be a valuable asset. There's a disconnect—person X who needs the skill, knowledge, or experience just doesn't know that person Y has what she needs. It is important for organizations to better leverage their resources—they have to create a viable system that allows people with the information to connect with those who need it. And they need forward-thinking leaders who understand the importance of sharing and leveraging information to create the framework that enables this environment.

The most effective networks are often informal—like-minded people start to chat, get to know each other, and find things in common—they begin to develop relationships. Yet most people don't even know what their colleagues do at work, let alone outside work. We created a network information sheet for a number of our clients to allow employees to find out interesting and pertinent information about each other. Employees share not only professional information but also personal interests, experience, and background, as well as their hobbies, the languages they speak, the countries they have lived in, their special talents, and sports—things they want others to know about them. It not only creates social networks but also makes everyday work more effective—you know who the "go-to person" is for your specific needs.

In order to develop networks of like-minded people to share and leverage knowledge, it is essential to find out who is out there, what they do, and what their interests are. In addition to providing a fresh perspective on a process or product, informal information networks often can bypass traditional formal communication lines and get to the real information.

The physical setting of a building also can foster this informal sharing. For example, 3M traditionally has put white boards along its corridors so that if people are discussing some innovation as they walk down the hall, they have a place to write down their ideas as they brainstorm. Some organizations set up informal seating areas throughout their space for colleagues to gather and chat as they informally run into each other during the day. Physically putting complementary functional areas, cross-functional brand teams, departments, or disciplines near each other can maximize their interaction, foster their networking, create stronger relationships, and enhance the possibility of generating interdisciplinary concepts and projects. As one CFO mentioned: "I don't golf. But I like to get together with people at work, put my feet up, and chat with them over a cup of coffee. It's a great way to get to know each other and get to know what they can do and how they think."

In addition to serving as a resource of people who have what you need, informal networks also provide a comfort level in sharing information among the members. If you have greater trust, you communicate on a different level—when they call, you get right back to them regardless of your day's demands. There's an instant rapport—you understand how they operate, there's an understanding of their style. This type of tacit knowledge found in informal networks exists in every organization—but how do people tap into it?

While explicit knowledge includes information that is written down, tacit knowledge is less tangible, harder to define.[2] In most organizations, the traditional, formal sources of information (explicit knowledge), such as minutes from meetings, announcements, press releases, annual reports, and so forth, usually are summarized and generated by more senior managers. Most employees probably are not either privy to or concerned with this information. (Ironically, if the information doesn't affect them directly in their jobs or doesn't appear to affect them, it is probably largely ignored by many employees despite the effort and cost put into disseminating it.) However, there is another source of information and knowledge going on at the same time, one that is part of the culture, a sort of underground network, a word of mouth—it's what people just know. This is tacit information. It's knowing who the right people are to go to for the information you need and it's the day-to-day way that things get done or who is doing the great new innovative stuff. The challenge is to bring these informal leaders together to create partnerships among informal leaders.

Ironically, senior management generally is not included in these exchanges—the ones that take place in the cafeteria or around the proverbial water cooler. However, when leaders need real-world feedback, suggestions for how to "do it better," identifying latent talent potential, or informal mentoring, these opportunities are extremely helpful. Leaders should be aware of how powerful these informal networks are and be anxious to participate. They can make opportunities to participate, for example, in informal brown bag lunches. Leaders can talk about a topic of interest to them, perhaps with 15 to 20 employees at a table in the cafeteria. There is no cost, just their time. Any group interested in informal leadership development can organize it, scheduling such an event once a month, perhaps, and asking various key leaders to participate just once. It's great for the employees—they get to hear and network with senior leaders. It's great for the leaders—they have the opportunity to get feedback and to see what the real issues are and perhaps do some informal mentoring. It is important to set an informal culture, an open forum in which people can discuss interesting and diverse topics. Good leaders want to be accessible and are open to listening to their employees in an informal environment. Seeing who your resources are—and knowing how to leverage them—is a great outcome for leaders. One senior leader shares:

> *When I participate in a small group discussion with more junior people, sometimes I just like to sit back and observe the interaction, see who's contributing, how people think, communicate, persuade. What new ideas are being generated—even off-the-wall ideas.*

CREATING A LEARNING COMMUNITY: ADDING VALUE, INCREASING PERFORMANCE

A number of our participants underscored the importance of leaders being able to learn. The world is changing too rapidly. Leaders can no longer just respond to change; they need to be able to anticipate it, adapt, be flexible, and change direction when necessary to meet market conditions, demands, and crises. Organizations need to foster collaboration. They need to work with people to improve their ability to share knowledge and to help them understand how they learn and how they use and share information and knowledge. For example, some people use online resources for general information. However, when they want to share knowledge, they count on their networks, their informal relationships. It is critical to understand how knowledge sharing happens naturally. It's people getting together and thinking, discovering, talking, sharing—and learning. But if you ask any leader, individuals with this combination of human capital and social capital are in high demand. Two leaders share their view on finding the right people for competitive advantage:

> *We need people who can work effectively in a matrix, people who can collaborate across the organizations. No one ever has all of the necessary organizational resources at their disposal, nor do they have every critical person reporting to them. You have to lead individuals who don't report to you—and get resources from others, as well. It needs to be a very relationship-oriented culture.*

ন৵১

> *Our organization is multidimensional based on geography, functions, processes, professions. . . . We need leaders who enable collaboration across boundaries, but who are also able to deliver results and accept accountability for their own areas of responsibility as well*

as for adding value to the greater organization. In other words, we want champions of an organizational community who can cast a shadow of influence and motivation beyond their own teams.

These groups, knowledge networks, are not necessarily focused on a particular task but on knowledge itself. They come together by way of shared knowledge—or search for knowledge—and a common sense of interest or purpose. These are people who are excited—and often passionate—about connecting with like-minded people, creating value, enabling innovation, and finding a solution. They can be employees in the same organization or industry who face common challenges or issues, or they can be colleagues in search of best practices or cross-disciplinary academics who find that they have research interests in common—knowledge networks can occur in many different settings.

The main challenge for any organization is to figure out how best to enable these communities. Some of the people we spoke to underscore that although their people may belong to a specific functional area, they must consider the needs of the organization as a whole—connecting with their colleagues both horizontally and vertically. The leaders that we have identified as EPIC leaders realize the importance of fostering a knowledge-sharing environment and are able to make these connections and see the big picture—essentially putting the right people together and not creating a redundancy in resources.

There's an interesting article highlighting a study conducted throughout a yacht race that reflects this topic. The skipper's leadership was a key element—what a great parallel to leadership in any organization! His ability to focus on strategies and implement mechanisms to create a knowledge-sharing culture enhanced the crew's performance and gave the team a competitive edge, leading to ultimate victory. In any highly competitive and challenging environment, leaders should model an openness and willingness to communicate. This skipper openly shared his own knowledge with the crew and was willing to try new sailing procedures offered by crewmembers. Exhibiting high levels of emotional intelligence—a belief in himself and his abilities—he accepted questioning from the crew, as well as upward feedback. Valuing the skills and experience of crewmembers from other walks of life, he was willing to change his behavior if the situation warranted it. When making decisions with insufficient information, he wasn't afraid to ask advice—isn't this a sign of a confident leader—not afraid of looking "weak" by inviting other points of view? Finally, clarity of direction and preparation were essential for these leaders—one skipper wrote a series of detailed papers for his team to better understand routines and activity sequences, whereas another even compiled a comprehensive manual of best practices for future races.[3]

CREATING A SUCCESSFUL KNOWLEDGE NETWORK

It is essential to understand how knowledge is created and shared in your environment, both internally and externally. Does your organization foster the type of environment that allows these networks to grow and flourish? Do leaders even know if there are any of these networks? These informal networks may be well served by identifying and seeking out someone— preferably at a high (and visible) level—to become a sponsor or champion of the group, raising visibility, giving advice, and possibly contributing resources and building support. A friend of ours, Gena McCleary, was such a champion at a leading pharmaceutical firm, and she did a fantastic job. Passionate, insightful, and high energy, she has a way of seeing the big picture, identifying people who share interests and goals, and bringing them together in a knowledge network, as well as having the connections and clout to make them visible.

However, it is important to keep at least some networks or communities of knowledge from becoming too formalized into the fabric of the organization. Many informal networks are enormously successful simply by virtue of the people in them. There is a common interest: great people, exciting and thought-provoking discussions, curiosity, interest in learning—and fun. Other, more formal networks can become bogged down with bylaws and legal restraints—they become too formal, too much time and energy are spent on the structure and not enough focus is placed on sharing. It just stops being fun and interesting. In these days of painfully little time, most individuals have to make choices about where they will find the greatest value for the time they invest. The group has to be innately interesting enough to consistently attract new members and keep people engaged, excited, and anxious to attend. However, bigger is not always better.

USING TECHNOLOGY IN KNOWLEDGE NETWORKS

Just because the information is out there (online, in a database, etc.) doesn't mean that people will use it. Sometimes technology is the best way to get knowledge, and sometimes not. For example, is it quicker (and better) to do an online search for background information on a potential new client, or can you just call a colleague who has worked with or for that client? It depends—do you need an overview of the organization or advice on the best way to pitch your product and to whom? It's all about knowing what and who is available in your knowledge network and effectively leveraging that information. And just because some people constantly use technology, particularly in their jobs, don't make assumptions about their learning styles. They might prefer other ways of learning. When engineers at one software company were to receive training, they wanted classroom instruction, not just e-learning. They actively sought out social interaction in the learning, which can drive creativity. Online knowledge wasn't enough. Spontaneous classroom interaction between instructors and learners and among learners is often an outstanding way to drive innovation.[4]

Technology also can be extremely effective with regard to information gathering and dissemination. Especially in our increasingly global environment, it allows and indeed encourages a global network. Information and access are essential not only to allow but also to encourage all employees to share information—to enhance dialogue. From a broader perspective, technology also can provide an excellent forum for building informal relationships. A plethora of online forums and chat rooms provides an informal platform that can result in an exchange of information, advice, and best practices. Likewise, other venues such as online classes can develop surprising communities of learning, including information sharing, advice, and informal mentoring. One leader adds:

We're using technology more and more as a means of learning, sharing information, connecting people. The challenge is in the more remote locations—bandwidth is a limitation, for example, in streaming video. A more interactive environment is very important. Those three people in the North Dakota office need to know as much as those in Manhattan; they need to be able to connect, so remote access is very important. However, the challenge is bringing along our employees who are less technology/Internet-friendly.

SHARING INFORMATION, LEVERAGING RESOURCES

We have heard the same observation from a number of people in organizations worldwide: "Unfortunately, we're not too good at leveraging the [human] resources at our firm." An important ingredient for successful organizations is the ability to leverage resources, maximizing the talent that they have and taking advantage of every opportunity for input into solving complex problems. Most organizations spend a great deal of time and money gathering and analyzing information pertaining to performance and results—how to do it better—that is often only available to the most senior managers. The remainder of the employees may see a homogenized, truncated version of the information that may be germane to what they do or perhaps only hear the "headlines" from their boss or others. How much information generated in such a process is wasted?

Information should be shared to create knowledge not only so that individuals at all levels can do their own job better but also to be able to collectively solve problems, generate an innovative new concept, or provide insights into how a process or service can be improved. There's the spark of connecting the dots—the "Aha!" or "Wait, I've gotten some interesting feedback on that from my customers" or "Some of my colleagues in the industry have had success with this" or "I heard about this at the last conference I attended, and there was a good discussion on best practices." Employees at all levels of the organization need to be privy to a lot more information. We're not talking about state secrets here, but a process for facilitating a more effective sharing of knowledge is needed—creating a system that allows for that process. It's about formal structure and informal networks and informal sources of information. Effective leaders know how to leverage their resources, cultivating relationships with a wide range of people, sharing information and ideas across the organization and beyond, and using technology to facilitate how they gather and share information. Most organizations have their own stories, from missed opportunities to critical errors owing to a lack of information. Now more than ever, organizations need as much access as possible to up-to-the-minute information.

Organizations sometimes can overlook their external networks as well. Not only do they need to listen to what end users want, but they also have to be creative and predict what end users will want in the future, anticipating and responding to emerging trends and buzz in the marketplace. One leader adds her insights:

We look five to ten years into the future to determine what competencies we will need in the future. We will need people who are comfortable working in alliances of corporate, academic, and political members. Leaders must learn to cross traditional boundaries to create virtual organizations. They must listen to stakeholders, understand how to make decisions and to reach agreement in this new environment.

Underscoring the importance of communication, organizations must solicit feedback from their end users to determine not only what they want but also how to provide better service, more options, or greater insight into what needs to be changed. A tremendously insightful and observant friend of ours, Govi, sat down with the senior management of an excellent hotel in Asia some years ago to conduct an evaluation of their service, an audit of sorts—which doesn't sound surprising, except that he was a guest at the time. Observing a number of issues that needed to be addressed, he spoke proactively to the hotel managers and set up a meeting. Far from being offended, the hoteliers eagerly sought out—and acted on—his feedback. If only all customers gave such insights!

BEST PRACTICES IN DEVELOPING INFORMAL NETWORKS

Before we undertook this research, we were asked by several of our clients: "So, what are other organizations doing to address such and such an issue?" Or "We're starting up several special interest groups at our company—do you know anyone doing the same type of thing?" Most organizations are challenged with understanding the scope—and critical importance—of developing these knowledge networks or communities of practice and the business consequences of not addressing the issue. In addition, they frequently may not even know where to begin—not to mention being able to invest the necessary time and energy to undertake this task. What can organizations do to enable and facilitate such communities?

At one end, many organizations may need to undertake a significant culture change process that can take years. However, it is critical to at least begin the process to enable people to get together in an informal yet somewhat structured environment. It can start with something as simple as just physically bringing the people together and encouraging the culture of sharing. At a financial services giant, employees in one functional area periodically host a "Night in Operations," simply an opportunity to get people from across the organization to join them socially for refreshments and chat about what's going on, what's new, and updates on projects and accomplishments—bringing people together to share ideas and to get to know each other.

Most organizations think that expensive (and often exclusionary) golf outings or other elaborate events that take months of planning are the only way to get people together to develop these key relationships. However, organizations should bring people together more frequently and less formally. Several organizations we spoke to hold cooking classes for their emerging leaders and senior management to get to know each other. Others host informal dinners with great thought leaders as speakers. Still other organizations take the opportunity to celebrate any milestone, just to bring people together. "The sales department just brought in a big new client—

join us for pizza at noon to help us celebrate." "Our IT department worked for two weeks straight to successfully launch our new system—they need a pickup. Join us for coffee and donuts for a caffeine and sugar jolt." The important thing is to have reasons to simply get people together (always with food, from what people tell us). Likewise, we have suggested to some organizations that they sponsor conferences or even informal luncheons with speakers on a topic of interest and invite customers, suppliers, and so on to join. It is important to bring together like-minded individuals, internal and external, to join in a discussion of common interest, as well as to network and socialize. Organizations get a better sense of what customers and other stakeholders are thinking, what the trends are, and what the buzz is. For example, a recent ASTD cocktail hour featured tables that were organized by areas of interest, such as global, technology, current challenges, and so forth, and identified by color-coded balloons and signs. People could immediately locate a group with a similar interest among hundreds of people. This simple design generated great conversation from the outset. An effort to bring colleagues together across industries, functions, global regions, and beyond can do a lot to let people discover each other and help a network or community come together naturally.

In addition, it is important to use whatever time people are together (especially if they don't come together often) to maximize networking. You have seen it—everyone comes into a session, program, or presentation from different parts of the organization—and no one talks to each other! Give them an "assignment"—tell them to get together with the two or three people around them and find three things in common. The room instantly comes alive with conversation, laughing, and sharing of stories. In these situations we have heard people connecting on new jobs—someone is looking for specific skills for an upcoming position—and the person chatting with them has those skills, and they agree to have lunch that week to talk. Future relationships are forged. A junior employee mentions that she is active with Habitat for Humanity, and a senior vice president adds, "Let's get together at the break and talk further—I've been wanting to get involved in that." Even including slightly longer session breaks to allow for the sharing of thoughts and getting to know each other can be valuable.

Targeted small group assignments and workshops can range from addressing specific issues or organizational challenges in small group exercises to organizing more formalized networks or communities of practice within the organization. One of the most common benefits we hear from events and activities that bring together high potentials, senior leaders, or others to address real-world organizational issues and challenges is not only the high energy and focused solutions but also the networking—especially on a global level. Our participants—from middle managers to the executive team—tell us that these "unanticipated outcomes" often can be as powerful as the formal presentations themselves. We hear the feedback at the end of programs or presentations that we conduct: "Everyone's favorite part was the networking—we are usually so busy working in silos that we don't make the time to get together and share." Leaders (and others) need to be aware of the power of enabling the culture—and creating opportunities—for people to share, connect, find common ground, and develop relationships. The outcome often can be innovation, feedback, shared knowledge, advice, mentoring, and a more encompassing community.

KNOWLEDGE SHARING—RISK AND REWARD

Leaders should determine how a knowledge-sharing environment can be established and nurtured at their organizations. What will be the goals, the process, and how will it be measured? What resources are available, internally and externally? Who is already working on it? How will the knowledge be gathered, evaluated, and tracked? However, many organizations are doing nothing to develop this knowledge-sharing environment. Why not? One major reason is the organizational culture. Innovation requires a certain mind-set that tolerates risk—and failure. If you're saying as a leader that you want to foster greater sharing of knowledge—and one of the outcomes from bringing together smart, motivated, and energetic people is that they're coming up with all kinds of new and exciting innovations—are you logistically and culturally prepared for that as an organization? Do you have all the necessary elements in place to enable that kind of a culture? In addition, many people don't see the value of networks—they think it's all about getting a job. Likewise, many people admit that they just don't make the time to do it—even though they know they should. They're on overload, just getting their day-to-day jobs done. There is also a certain element of trust—individuals are sharing their own knowledge. Is the person to whom they are entrusting it going to respect that relationship with integrity? There's risk involved in sharing your knowledge with others.

In order to create this knowledge-sharing environment, you need a culture in which this open discussion, networking, and sharing of knowledge can take place—and this culture comes from the top. Leaders have to know how knowledge flows throughout the organization, internally (across functions, globally, etc.) as well as externally (customers, colleagues, suppliers, etc.). It is also critical that these leaders be able to connect the dots, bring the pieces together, ask the right questions, understand the big picture, and appreciate the importance of sharing knowledge. Essentially, they should be thinking, "Wait a minute, I know that so-and-so is doing this, and I think that we can work with her to make our task easier, more efficient, and more productive or our product/service more competitive. . . . Let's start talking." As a result, organizations can create leaner processes and can achieve better coordination of organizational functions (especially cross-functionally or globally), greater leveraging of resources for competitive advantage, and greater innovation, more creativity, better solutions, increased market share, greater productivity, and reduced costs.

CHAPTER SUMMARY
Success Secret #3: Managing Your Knowledge Networks

♦ The knowledge economy requires—and enables—24/7 access, allowing greater sharing of information and knowledge worldwide and fostering innovation and greater productivity.

♦ The emphasis in this environment is not on knowledge itself but on using it and leveraging it for greater competitive advantage.

♦ Future organizational performance will be tied not only to human capital—what people bring to organizations—but also to social capital—who they know.

♦ Organizations—and individuals—need to move from keeping knowledge to themselves to sharing knowledge across networks to enable greater creativity and innovation. Organizations must examine how to better enable these informal networks.

♦ Technology has increased access to knowledge worldwide exponentially through the Internet, e-mail, and inexpensive telephony, among other things.

Author note: There are several different aspects/levels of knowledge sharing that readers should be aware of. While knowledge networks are generally looser and more informal than communities of practice, which potentially lead to communities of commitment, we are choosing to underscore the importance of the *concept* without going into great detail about the primary and at times subtle differences among them. We may subsequently use terms interchangeably. However, since there are different elements and strategies for use that are unique and specific to each, we would suggest that practitioners interested in further definition or a greater depth of the topic explore some of the many excellent resources that go into those differences.

In addition, various measures are available to map this informal flow of information and knowledge—who is talking to whom, who is influencing whom, and who is seeking information. They can give a sense of individual and team roles in these informal networks—where knowledge is coming from and going to, who is part of the network and what roles they may play, and who are the key thought leaders, experts, knowledge brokers, and influencers. Different from an organizational chart that displays formal reporting structures, these approaches track relationships among people.

For more information, the *Journal of Social Structure* (JoSS) is an electronic journal of the International Network for Social Network Analysis (INSNA).

Persuading, Influencing, and Communicating Your Vision

ᴼᴸᴼ

I can't overemphasize the role that strong communication skills play. Leaders must be able to explain to all the organization's stakeholders what is going on in the business and to articulate where the enterprise is and what its needs are. To do this, leaders must demonstrate strong technical skills and a thorough understanding of a wide range of elements, particularly the finance role. People want someone who can answer the question, "What is the story behind the numbers?" And those outside the organization are desperate to hear leaders be candid about their organization—not pompous.

One of the realities of leading in today's flatter organizations is that leaders must communicate, persuade, and inspire—people want leaders who have an innate ability to bring people together and to motivate them to get things done. They have a self-awareness, they limit their egos, and they listen to their people. Great leaders have an aura of confidence about them; they reassure, and they create an energy around them, letting their people know that they care about them. These leaders create a sense of excitement and enthusiasm around them—that "things are going to happen, and I want to be a part of it." And it's a good thing that they have this going for them—because another reality is that, more times than not, they don't have power over the people on their teams. All they can do is influence and persuade. But don't get the impression that all these "new leaders" are soft, overly emotionally intelligent pushovers. Far from it. It's just that they know how to read the crowd and read the context. We've seen chief executive officers (CEOs) who are tough as nails with their senior executives at one moment and casually chatting with the employees in the cafeteria the next. Great leaders know how to be flexible and adaptable. They know what style is going to work with a given group— and which style won't.

Part of this comes from a keen understanding of the people with whom they are communicating. They have learned that there is no one correct style—they wear many hats. When they're talking to the workers on the shop floor, it's different than when they are representing the organization at a charity fund-raiser. However, the message needs to be the same and always consistent. They are sharing the vision of the organization, the passion for what they are all doing there, and how they all play a part in that vision.

COMMUNICATING YOUR VISION

One of the key challenges leaders have is communicating to the organization what they want to do—their vision. One executive at a global financial institution told us that as he visits the offices worldwide, he can chat with people in the mailroom, and they will be able to articulate at least two or three points in the organizational vision and say how it relates to them and how they apply it in their everyday jobs. Likewise, if you talk to employees at Johnson & Johnson, they know the credo—they can tell you what it means to them; they live it every day. At some colleges, the vision is so engrained in the institution that the groundskeepers not only can tell you what it is, but they also can tell you their role in it. What is it about these and other organizations like them that enables their employees to so clearly understand their vision? It's a vision that's memorable. Their people know it and internalize it. They're able to articulate it. If people can't do this, you haven't made your vision clear enough. It needs to be simple and clear—they need to know how it applies to them and how they can make a difference in the big picture. They should be able to tell you what it is and how it applies to them in their own words. It should get people excited.

Leaders must set and articulate a clear vision. They need to inspire and motivate—to make it a challenge, a stretch. They need to set a passionate example. However, at any given time, the CEO should focus only on five to six strategic goals—the critical issues in the organization, the key factors in the value proposition, the performance drivers. However, senior executives should be working closely with their direct reports to continually articulate how what their team members are doing is delivering on those goals— they're guiding the execution.

How clearly do your leaders communicate their vision and inspire their followers to embrace it? Our guess is that although most organizations have a vision statement, most employees don't have a clue as to what it says, let alone how they play a role in achieving it. What good is a vision—and how can you achieve it quickly and globally—if no one even knows what it is? Employees at every level need to see the connection between where the organization is going and what role they play individually and collectively in that journey.

PERSUASION

We want individuals who are going to be great ambassadors—those who can articulate why we're a great firm to a wide range of different constituents.

Leaders need to build consensus, gain buy-in, and solicit feedback. They need to bring people together—often those from a wide range of functional areas and industries, as well as customers, suppliers, partners, and shareholders. They need to keep everyone motivated, informed, and focused on strategic goals. They need to resolve conflict and come to consensus—or at least a good solution—all without saying, "We're doing this because I'm telling you to." Situations can run the gamut—a shareholders' meeting, a cross-functional team, a high-level negotiation, or a meeting with external partners to work on a new project. However, these leaders don't do it alone. They solicit help from informal influential leaders across the organization and beyond.

In Chapter 3 we talked a lot about tacit knowledge—that informal "underground network" that exists in every organization—the people who have all the "inside information" that's going on, those who have all the answers to your questions. Likewise, all organizations have networks of influential leaders—the people who have influence within these informal networks. They're the ones of whom everyone asks advice and goes to for guidance. They're leaders in their field or area of expertise, they have earned the respect of others, they evoke trust and confidence, and they have credibility. What is it about these people? The ones who come to mind all have different personalities—some are outgoing and some reserved. They come from various backgrounds and don't necessarily have what most would think are "prestigious" degrees or positions. Not all influential leaders are even found at the top. But they have something—it's subtle—a confident expertise, the persona that they have something worthwhile to say, albeit occasionally controversial, but they can back it up and persuade you to their reasoning. Of course, there's always the possibility that they will challenge the status quo or support exactly the opposite of what you want to do. Therefore, if they're smart, leaders will get a sense early on whether the high-influence individuals support or oppose their views on change and then work on maximizing opportunities to persuade them.

> *Senior leaders have big egos. If you're a new member of the team—whether through promotion or external recruitment—you can't "blow up" the previous work of that team and then ask for their help to move your own projects forward.*

Building a network of these influential leaders can allow senior leaders to get the pulse point of key constituents. Such a network also will allow emerging leaders to get personal feedback and enable them to share their views on issues, challenges, and possible solutions, as well as get a sense of what's going on in other industries, professions, and organizations.

More and more frequently, team leaders have far less actual control over their team than in the past. You can't hire, fire, or discipline them—you can only use your influence. It may be an international team or a cross-functional work group that doesn't report to you, a team of outside vendors, or a group of individual projects coming together under you. Looking forward, the organization of the future is virtual, where nontraditional, internal, and external partnerships are created. It's a challenge to get them to do what you want—and need—them to do.

One executive shares his experience in influencing those over whom he has no formal authority:

> *Be confident, but not arrogant—don't put yourself in a role where you are perceived as a threat or a usurper. It also helps to get the CEO's ear, ensuring that he/she heeds that advice—and for the troops to know that. But it is also important to spend time with your team members, asking them about their jobs, their difficulties and frustrations, and what can be done to help them do their jobs better—don't be overtly judgmental. Most workers respond to someone who not only listens, but also someone who actually does something about it—leaders who consider it their responsibility to help their team members do their jobs better.*

It's important to remember that good leadership is not based on a title or formal authority. As many of the leaders we interviewed agreed, it's a matter of trust and respect, which are earned over time. In order for leaders to have good "followship," they need to listen thoughtfully to team members' ideas, be truthful and admit mistakes, work hard, show integrity, and ask for input from team members. Emotional intelligence is a key element of persuasion—not having a controlling personality, an "ego." One of our participants provides an example:

Leaders who apply soft skills get their people to move mountains. They should also be willing to "get their hands dirty"—leading by example.

It is also essential that leaders establish clear goals and objectives for the team. As one participant explains: "We have to articulate a set of expectations—what it is that we want people to do to meet our strategic agenda. We also have to be systematic in identifying who represents those capabilities—who stands out." In addition, many of our participants do some serious homework on assigning team member tasks, aligning them with the capabilities and interests of the members—if people are excited about the task, little persuasion will be required. Leaders need to get a sense of how things are going during the process through open discussion, not necessarily by asking for progress reports. If they're the gold-collar workers whom you really want to have on the team to get the best results or solutions, they are just as likely to be creative thinkers who focus on the results, not the process. They will balk at too much micromanaging. The team culture should be one of open sharing, encouragement, dialogue, and feedback. Or as one leader says, "Leaders not only need to give feedback, but to receive it non-defensively." Another participant puts it a different way: "Our leaders should be intellectually honest—willing to debate in an open way."

Leaders agree that given the talent in today's organizations, most managers, of necessity, increasingly must lead by persuasion—younger high potentials especially won't tolerate a controlling environment. Managers and team leaders want to maximize their talent, their diverse perspectives, and their knowledge. Management by persuasion, or lateral leadership, as some people call it, is often an excellent way to optimize this potential. And, they say, this approach can be learned. The best leaders have people who want to follow—they don't have to be directive. One of our participants articulates this concept:

When I think about what makes people successful, it's a combination of super intellect and great lateral leadership skills—relationship skills, influence skills. However, intellect will only take them so far. Relationship and influence skills take them on from there. They have to be able to "rally the troops" with their passion.

Another major aspect of communication is listening, although many leaders of the past may not have realized it. Today, many of our leaders overwhelmingly cite the importance of listening as a critical leadership skill. Leaders must be interested in others—and what they have to say. They have to be curious and empathetic. As a leader—and we're talking leadership at all levels, from leading your first small team to CEO—one needs to be a dynamic, active listener, asking questions, gathering information, talking to customers to see what they have to say, and talking to employees to hear their issues. It's what most talented employees expect—and they will subtly remind leaders of this point—if they don't like your organizational culture, they'll go somewhere else. Good leaders know that buy-in and collaboration are essential to making things happen, and listening to the needs and perspectives of customers, employees, and others is key. You need to get at the pulse point of what people want.

COMMUNICATING IN A CRISIS

Nowhere is the need for outstanding communication skills more critical than in times of crisis. Here are a couple of examples that express this sentiment:

Any time you're in a crisis, the communications level has to be stepped up, in our case it was principally by e-mail. You want to let your people know specifically what is going on. There were messages from the CEO, and I sent many messages to my team. People believe that you care more when you communicate the situation with them— they really appreciate it. You also need to communicate about four or five times more than you normally do. Your visibility is key to confidence.

ᴄⱱᴏ

It is important for all leaders to show a genuine interest in the health, welfare, and well-being of their staff—you can't fake it. Inherent to changing an organization is the possibility of reorganizations and layoffs. Be upfront and honest as much as possible. I believe that "employees can take bad news." The problem comes when the employees see the bureaucracy at work, with all the discussions going on behind closed doors, but nothing being disclosed. In a reorganization, there is a vacuum of information. It fills with either fact or rumor. Communicating as much as possible (without, of course, revealing sensitive information) takes away a lot of the anxiety.

PUBLIC SPEAKING AND WRITING SKILLS: ESSENTIAL FOR SUCCESSFUL LEADERS

Another key leadership skill expressed by a number of our participants was the importance of developing presentation and public speaking skills. One of the things that we have heard a lot from leaders is the importance of their public image when they communicate. They reflect the company—no, they *are* the company to the public. When you hear about major crises at most companies, who speaks at the press conference or gives the interviews on networks, and who talks to the shareholders? The top leaders. When Ford was faced with its tire nightmare on Explorers, whom did you see? Jacques Nasser. When Chrysler had to be turned around? Lee Iacocca. The Microsoft trial? Bill Gates. And many others during the September 11 tragedy. In fact, leaders at all levels find themselves in the public eye every day—communicating with Wall Street analysts, with shareholders, with their employees, and with customers. But being in the public eye comes as a rude awakening for many leaders when they find themselves faced with this issue for the first time. One CEO shares his experience:

There is one serious skill investment I made later in my career than I should have: developing and honing my public speaking, presentation, and video skills. Most executives never find the time to really improve and believe they are just fine on camera or behind the podium. As we all know, most of them are wrong—painfully wrong.

So how do you learn? First of all, assume that you will need to be more in the public eye as your career advances—either internally or externally, you will be speaking more in front of people. Did you think that a career in accounting or technology would protect you from it? Think again if you want to advance in your organization. But does the prospect of presenting in front of a group strike fear into your heart? It does for many people. As with most things, though, you need to practice and get advice and training from professionals. One executive shared his thoughts with us during a conference presentation. A senior vice president for a major technology corporation, he did the kickoff keynote for the day. We've rarely seen anything like it—not as much as an index card in his hand as he spoke to 200 people for almost an hour. And he didn't just talk to them—he engaged them, he was funny, he was articulate, he was prepared, and he followed a theme. We talked to him after the break and complimented him on his outstanding presentation. He just laughed and said, "Oh, thanks—but I have to admit, I couldn't sleep most of last night because I was so worried about this. I am very nervous speaking in front of people." We were amazed. And of course, we asked him how he did it? He took presentation and public speaking classes and practiced whenever he could. It obviously worked! Another executive shares his thoughts:

As you become a leader, your skills need to grow as you grow into bigger and bigger jobs. Public speaking, for example, became more important for me—especially in Asia. I did a presentation a week in front of thousands of people. As a finance guy, I had to overcome that apprehension.

Many senior leaders across industries find themselves dealing with the same issues. For example, when a group of the most senior women in the country went to the Breakers in Palm Beach for a networking weekend, what was one of the topics? Speaking to the media, to analysts on Wall Street, and to the shareholders. For many leaders, it's a new skill that must be learned and practiced. Likewise, we spoke a few years ago to the National Association of Women Legislators, a group of relatively new members of Congress, lieutenant governors, and so forth. A major focus of the week? Public speaking. Ask any senior person at your organization—he will agree. It is absolutely critical to develop these public speaking skills.

Although communication skills always have been paramount for successful leaders, there are some new considerations that should be kept in mind. As business becomes more global, communication styles have to be adapted. Does the culture you're working in demand a formal style, or is a casual approach acceptable? Are you speaking and writing in a way that is clear and comprehensible for an audience that may not share your native language—are you using idioms and contexts that are not understood by all cultures?

In addition, the overwhelming preference for electronic communication brings its own problems. Many companies are organizing writing classes that are available to all employees but particularly current and emerging leaders. Many people lack basic writing skills to convey a clear, unambiguous message. No matter how brilliant the idea, it is diminished by poor grammar, spelling, and composition. And when leaders want to communicate with remote team members, clients, and other audiences, they further must be able to write persuasively and with authority. Don't forget too that these communications are now part of the public record—you never know to whom the message will be forwarded or who is on the distribution list. It is important to be ethically and legally responsible when sending electronic mail. Don't overlook internal and external resources for help—human resources, corporate communications, or your local community colleges, among others, if you feel that you or your team members could benefit from communications support.

CHAPTER SUMMARY
Success Secret #4: Persuading, Influencing, and Communicating Your Vision

♦ Leaders in today's flatter organizations must communicate, persuade, inspire. People want leaders who have an innate ability to bring people together and motivate them to get things done.

♦ Great leaders create a sense of excitement and enthusiasm around them—that "things are going to happen, and I want to be a part of it."

♦ Leaders have to understand with whom they are communicating. There is no one correct style—it's different when they are talking to workers on the shop floor than when they are representing the organization at a charity fund-raiser. However, the message always needs to be consistent.

♦ Leaders must set and articulate a clear vision and inspire and motivate to make it a challenge, a stretch. They must set a passionate example. However, at any given time, the CEO should focus on only five to six strategic goals—the critical issues in the organization, the key factors in the value proposition, and the performance drivers.

♦ Leaders need to build consensus, gain buy-in, and solicit feedback. They must bring people together from a wide range of functional areas and industries, as well as customers, suppliers, partners, and shareholders.

♦ For leaders to have good "followship," they must listen to and ask for input from team members, be truthful, admit mistakes, work hard, and show integrity. Emotional intelligence is a key element of persuasion, not having a controlling personality, an "ego."

♦ Leaders facing crisis should step up the communication level and convey a calm, confident attitude in verbal and nonverbal communication. They should seek out and focus on positive events and messages.

♦ Developing and honing public speaking, presentation, and video skills (in person, on camera, or behind the podium) is essential to leaders.

♦ As business becomes more global, communication styles must be adapted—formal style or casual approach commensurate with culture, speaking and writing that is clear and comprehensible for nonnative speakers, and avoiding idioms and contexts unfamiliar to the audience or people of different cultures.

♦ No matter how brilliant the idea, it is diminished by poor grammar, spelling, and composition. Leaders and future leaders may need to improve basic writing skills. Likewise, since leaders need to communicate with remote team members, clients, and other audiences, they must be able to write persuasively and with authority. Electronic mail communications are now part of the public record and must be written accordingly.

Creating a Culture of Integrity and Values

ov

Integrity is so integral to who we are and so vital to our every-
day operations that every employee here has a mouse pad
with our Pledge to Clients on it—an eight-point credo about
our commitment to clients. And right at the top is this: "We
continually seek to earn your trust and loyalty by adhering to
the highest standards of ethical behavior and fiduciary
responsibility. "You simply can't miss it. We have an uncom-
promising view of the importance of ethics and character in
our leadership team. It is nonnegotiable.

ORGANIZATIONAL VALUES AND INTEGRITY

Enron, WorldCom, Tyco, Adelphia, and Andersen. Just a few short years ago
these companies were being heralded as the companies to emulate, the best,
the ones whose stock you wanted to own, and the companies that case studies were written about. What a difference a few years make. From the pin-
nacle of success to the antithesis of integrity and trust, these companies
essentially mark the transition from the old world of business to the new.
Whereas at the new millennium soaring stock prices and corporate excesses
reigned supreme, now we're in the era of total disclosure and the Sarbanes-
Oxley Act. Most organizations have been forced to address questionable
issues head on. A more sobering—and most would say ethical—culture
has emerged in organizations worldwide.

Today, market forces and public expectations are driving the creation of
new rules. The emphasis is on corporate legitimacy, environmental preser-
vation, equity, diversity, ethical performance, and values.[1] Social responsibility is especially important on a global basis—people want to know what
you're doing to be a better global citizen, to make the world a better place.

There are higher expectations of organizations' values on the part of the public. Many organizations probably would not have taken action to the degree that they have if there had not been a heightened public awareness of the issue. Not that such organizations aren't concerned about the issues and run a tight ship. However, many organizations still believe that these soft areas, such as social responsibility, should not supersede competitive market advantage and shareholder value. Companies that underscored the importance of social values, such as The Body Shop or socially responsible investment firms, were on the fringes 10 years ago. However, with today's changing public sentiment, organizational values and integrity are at the heart of the best organizations. Shareholders want to deal with organizations they can trust. Likewise, next-generation leaders are looking for values in sync with their own. These superstars are asking questions in interviews about social responsibility and organizational values. They want an organizational culture that values not only hard work but also flexibility and a life beyond just work. They want a more holistic attitude.

In one survey, 88 percent of young people said that companies have a responsibility to support social causes—and that they also would switch brands to another associated with a social issue. Employee morale and increased scrutiny by consumers, investors, community activists, and employees have contributed to this new culture.[2]

More and more, leaders are reflecting on and defining their individual and organizational values and culture. When we asked our participants to share with us their thoughts on what they were looking for in current and next-generation leaders, the vast majority mentioned—unsolicited—such things as integrity, values, and ethical behavior. These are on almost everyone's agenda. As one leader commented, "Personal integrity has to do with having the courage to do the right thing. Leaders need to be willing to raise issues—in the right way—but raise them nonetheless." However, some leaders have put integrity at the forefront of their entire organizational culture. And in these cases it's not in response to regulatory oversight—it comes from the soul. These leaders believe in it unreservedly; they live it, model it, and expect it from others. KPMG Chief Executive Officer (CEO) Eugene O'Kelly talks about his firm's commitment to walking the walk:

> *One of our greatest challenges is to continue to rebuild the credibility of the accounting profession and for KPMG to be recognized by our professionals and the external marketplace as a great place to advance the careers of individuals in a rewarding environment. Earlier this year, we underscored our commitment to building exemplary leaders beyond our own firm by establishing the Global*

Initiative on Leadership and Business Ethics. Inspired by the spirit of the Nobel Prizes, the three-pronged program is aimed at recognizing outstanding business leaders. Its key components include KPMG as the Global Founding Partner of the Nobel Peace Center; KPMG's founding of The Global Center for Leadership & Business Ethics; and The Laureate Award & Medal Series, which recognizes outstanding individual or corporate achievement in business ethics and leadership qualities.

Social awareness is an enormously important global issue. For a variety of reasons, organizations are taking up the challenge and addressing social issues in record numbers. Pfizer sponsors the Pfizer Global Health Fellows (nicknamed Hank's Peace Corps for CEO Hank McKinnell), which is comprised of 30 skilled professionals loaned by the company to work with aid groups in developing countries for up to six months. Avon's breast cancer programs provide research, medical equipment, and mammograms in 50 countries. General Electric has committed $20 million to build hospitals in Africa. Xerox's Social Service Leave Initiative allows 3- to 12-month service leaves in which employees can decide where they want to volunteer their time at a functioning nonprofit—at full-time pay. Citigroup offers grants for small loans to 900,000 women in India alone. IBM sponsors a global on-demand community, an Intranet site allowing IBM volunteers to work on projects such as rewiring classrooms. Merck, Nike, the Bill and Melinda Gates Foundation, and dozens more are committed to these and other projects.[3]

Why the increased interest in philanthropy? First, of course, it's a good thing to be a responsible global citizen. However, it is possible to integrate corporate citizenship into sound business practices as well. Corporate observers emphasize that many of these countries represent new business markets and production centers for their companies—corporate revenues are increasingly coming from abroad as well. In many world regions where relationships play an important role in doing business, being a good global citizen helps when setting up shop in emerging countries—they already know and accept you. The concept of organizations enhancing life in less developed regions is not lost on the people in those regions in terms of loyalty to the organizations spearheading the efforts. From a different perspective, activists are increasingly urging companies to address social issues. Other companies want to augment their reputations globally, either to ameliorate a tarnished image or to keep possible critics at bay.

We have talked to several key leaders themselves about their own commitment to philanthropy. We were invited to join the CEO's walk at Unisys for a United Way kickoff—after hosting the rally for the campaign, the CEO led hundreds of employees on a walk throughout the corporate campus to promote the campaign. Likewise, Accenture leaders plan to highlight International Women's Day, and the festivities will include an opportunity for employees worldwide to spend that afternoon doing volunteer work for women as an element of the celebration.

Many organizations are publicly underscoring their commitment to philanthropy, and their leaders are spearheading the movement. These organizations and many others are making a clear and visible stand on how they are viewed by the outside world. However, organizations also need to take a tough look at their organizational culture. Is it one of inclusion, tolerance, open-mindedness, networks, shared resources, shared values, and integrity? Or does it include competition, exclusion, and questionable moral integrity?

ORGANIZATIONAL CULTURE

Increasingly, employees want a culture that is more flexible and more in keeping with their personal and professional needs. Many organizations are still wrestling with issues of balance—ironically, the very technology that makes many of our jobs easier and more flexible (home offices, e-mail, laptops, Blackberries, voice mail, global videoconferencing, and more) is also giving us less "time off." We live in an increasingly 24/7 world. Organizations, therefore, should be aware of their role in enabling a culture in which employees can feel a distinction between work life and "outside work" life. Many firms have instituted family-friendly initiatives, accommodating parents with childcare, flextime, and so forth—and that's fantastic. However, many of the people we talk to don't have kids, or their kids are older, but they are still looking for the same consideration. They're going to school, getting a degree, want to exercise to reduce stress, want to do volunteer work or give back to their community, and want to travel or actually go on vacations—they want to have a life! It is the responsibility of the senior leadership to model behavior that enables a culture that can effectively combine hard work with time to oneself.

Many of the leaders we spoke to talked about the importance of supporting such an environment. Most CEOs, granted, do have far more demanding schedules than the rest of us, but that doesn't necessarily mean that they don't have an outside life. One senior executive we interviewed volunteers for Meals on Wheels. A number of others added that they coach kids' sports—and we're talking CEOs here. The concept that executives just give lots of money but no time is not necessarily true. An organization is characterized by the leaders' values, the standard they set, the culture they engender, the decisions they make, the people they select, and their commitment to making things happen. Organizations need to decide who they want to be and what they want to become. And keep in mind—the organization is the people. If you want to gauge the culture of an organization, look around to see the makeup of teams and the people in key positions. It's probably a pretty accurate barometer despite what the public relations department is saying. Not too long ago we were looking at the annual report of one European corporation—it had a very nice photograph of senior management. Suffice it to say that the only diversity in the photo was that one of the white men in the photograph didn't have gray hair. That tells us something about the culture without turning the page. (We also know people there, and our observations were verified.) Conversely, part of the culture that so many of our research participants talked about was one of inclusion, diversity, different perspectives, and different approaches. When looking to change the culture dramatically and develop values that are in line with customers, clients, and supply chain partners, organizations need to start with their leadership—not only present leadership, but future leadership as well. One senior executive shares his views:

Managing across diverse businesses, cultures, and geographies is a major challenge. There are tensions between different geographies in a global firm—some are natural because of different backgrounds and perspectives; others are exacerbated by external political tensions. I believe finding common ground around the organization's mission and values is the key. . . . We need to embrace diversity without divisiveness and stay focused on a shared vision of success, which is how we create value and deliver results to our clients and people, and on a common set of values, which is what we stand for and how we behave as an institution. I believe this is the mark of enduring institutions—they create value and are based on values.

So many of the leaders we spoke to were fantastic—with their enthusiasm, their commitment, their energy, and their genuine concern for their people. It was energizing for us during the interviews, so we can imagine what it's like to be around them every day. Of course, some skeptics may say that anyone can portray a certain image for an hour to make themselves look good, but we heard the exact same sentiments from people who *do* work with them—"They're great!" However, while some organizations are fortunate enough to have had these insightful, future-focused leaders in terms of culture for quite some time, other leaders told us that they have gone through a relatively recent "epiphany" themselves, which has led them to a totally different way of leading. Now many of these leaders are also committed to encouraging this culture beyond their tenure; they are attracting and preparing the next generation of leaders.

Most organizations know that they need not only to recruit and retain talent but also to maintain a culture that is compatible with these future leaders' values. These young superstars won't stay where they're not happy and challenged. They value flexibility and opportunities for interesting and challenging work. They value social responsibility, community involvement, and workplace initiatives that suit their expectations. Some ego issues may be possible, but organizational systems may need to be addressed to reduce the prima donna behavior. Leaders should encourage working in teams that are assessed on several levels—not only individual recognition and reward systems but also performance appraisals based on team performance, as well as on efforts to develop future leaders.

These young leaders want bosses/leaders who are role models in terms of values, vision, goals, and charisma. They want leaders to challenge them to achieve more—to set high standards. They are looking at the culture of the organization, and they want it to be more informal and flexible, with an emphasis on hard work and an awareness of time for personal pursuits and opportunities for experiential learning and work on world-class projects. These future leaders are looking for workplace initiatives that fulfill their needs on many levels. For leaders in many organizations, this is a natural evolution. However, for many leaders with longer tenure, particularly in more hierarchical organizations, it is a 180-degree shift from the world of work they started in a generation or more ago. One of two things has to happen for organizations to make this inevitable transition and accommodate a new environment of work. Either the senior leadership has to respond to internal and external demands and start to make the necessary changes now, or the next generation of leaders, the ones a level or two below the executive team, need to start identifying other influential future leaders who "get it" and start putting the process in motion. One can be implemented more immediately; the other requires a more strategic long-term horizon. Obviously, it's easier if it's CEO-driven—but either way, it has to be done to attract and retain the necessary talent for the organization's future well-being.

CODE OF CONDUCT, CODE OF ETHICS

While a code of ethics or corporate conduct is required in some industries, what does it signify for most organizations? For many organizations, our guess is that it's a long legal document that includes every possible permutation of any possible scenario regarding organizational conduct, with multiple addendums as situations arise or the legal department envisions future problems. Yes, it is the proverbial CYA (cover your ... backside) document. A friend of ours, the chief administrative officer for a financial firm, mentioned that he is just about to overhaul his company's code of ethics with the company lawyers. When asked if anyone ever used it, he said, "Sure, we use it every day—it's a very well-read document. Everyone in our industry has to have one, and everyone needs to have access to it—internally and externally." We asked him, "What if someone has a question about a stock trade or what could be considered ethical or unethical behavior—are they able to get an answer quickly?" He said, "Everyone has a copy, but they usually just ask me." So it's still just a legal document. Organizations need to decide the purpose of such a statement. For one thing, where is your organizational code of ethics or code of conduct? Is it included in vision statements, in brochures, online, or on file somewhere in the legal department? Does anyone ever even look at it or know what it says? Does the code reflect global issues, and is it translated accurately to capture the real meaning? Is it easy to read so that employees and others actually can understand it, or does it resemble an incomprehensible legal document?

However, in some organizations, the code of conduct/code of ethics is more than the requisite legal CYA document. It's out there, and people actually know what it says. It represents an inspiring and shared vision underscored by the leaders. UBS features its "Visions and Values Document" clearly on its Web site. General Electric's "Statement of Integrity, the Spirit and the Letter of Our Commitment from CEO Jeffrey Immelt" encourages everyone to make a personal commitment to the code of conduct. Citigroup has a brief, clear, and colorful outline on its Web site, including six components of "what we value." The first heading is "Integrity." If there is going to be buy-in on an enterprise-wide level, it needs to be incorporated into everyday life and practice. Vanguard puts its "Pledge to Clients" on employee mouse pads to constantly reinforce their commitment. PriceWaterhouseCoopers has a comprehensive, highly attractive "Global Ethics" Web page that underscores every possible aspect of its code of conduct. Everyone at Johnson & Johnson's knows the company credo—it's what the organization is based on. Ernst & Young has a readable and great-looking 24-page online "Global Code of Conduct" that begins with a personal letter from its chief executive officer (CEO) and includes where/to whom to go for any clarification. These and many other organizations actually get it.

Why do we point out some of these codes of conduct, codes of ethics? Most organizations have excellent, comprehensive documents that outline every possible aspect of ethical conduct—but that's the point, they're documents, most likely put together very comprehensively by the legal department. But they're not a living, breathing guide to everyday values, attitudes, actions, and decisions with input from across the organization. Things like integrity, tolerance, courage, dignity, good citizenship, social responsibility. That's what makes up the culture—global buy-in, walking the walk, not a CYA document.

One of the things that we have been hearing more frequently from our clients and research participants is the idea of "tough decisions being made"—specifically with regard to great performers with poor attitudes. Organizations are increasingly looking at the whole picture—what kind of culture do we have, and what messages are we sending? Senior leadership is taking a stand and saying more and more, "Shape up or ship out." It's a very tough call, but leaders are starting to make it.

POWER OF ORGANIZATIONAL CULTURE/CORPORATE CULTURE/VALUES

Jim Collins, in his book *Good to Great,* observes that "companies that succeed long term stick to a set of values and create systems that get employees to act in accord with those values."[4] However, it's not enough to put it into your mission statement—people need to be able to recite it and live it. Leaders need to create systems to match organizational values and encourage/enable the right kind of employee behavior. They have to create the right environment and involve the right processes for selection, appraisal, job assignment, team creation, and mentoring. You find and hire the people who share your values. "You've got to walk the talk. If there is ambiguity about your message or values, people will opt out."

CHAPTER SUMMARY

Success Secret #5: Creating a Culture of Integrity and Values

♦ Whereas socially responsible organizations and others were on the fringes a decade ago, a more ethical culture has emerged in organizations worldwide.

♦ Employees and other stakeholders, internal and external, have higher expectations of organizations; they want to know what they're doing to be better global citizens.

♦ Future leaders especially are looking for organizations in sync with their values—a more holistic environment—hard work but flexibility and an emphasis on social responsibility and life beyond just work.

♦ Organizations worldwide have undertaken extensive philanthropy not only to improve life around the world but also as a sound business practice. These countries represent new business markets and production centers for their companies. Good relationships and a good reputation as a good global citizen help when establishing a presence.

♦ Organizations need to create a more comprehensive, user-friendly code of conduct/code of ethics if they wish to develop a culture that lives and breathes that code.

Leading in a Diverse Environment

cɪɔ

When I first took on a leadership role, I always seemed to see things that no one else saw, and would often have a very different perspective on the problem or solution. I thought that meant I was the one missing the big picture. I finally realized that, because I was different, I brought a new perspective to viewing the issue. I should have seen that my different way of analyzing the problem, and finding an alternative solution that took a different path to achieve the goal—was a value I added.

In its simplest sense, *diversity* can be defined as a difference of our perspectives and experience. But we are influenced to a great deal by a number of factors: culture, ethnicity, race, gender, age, sexual orientation, disabilities, and even the region in which we live. And each of these characteristics carries a set of values, beliefs, and behaviors that may seem foreign to others.

Some organizations avoid putting the diversity spotlight on a group of individuals but prefer to celebrate the diversity of thought that results from bringing together those with different backgrounds and experiences. Rather than focusing on diversity initiatives per se, they integrate the value of diversity into all elements of their leadership models. Our participants shared their views on the advantages that inclusiveness brings to the decision-making process.

Leaders have to be ready to challenge their own ideas on a given subject. Better solutions come from having a diverse team looking at the issue from different horizons and sharing ideas. Most organizational

problems are not logical or mathematical—where you program a computer and get the same information back every time. When I am working with a team, I like to be able to say, "Aha, now that's an interesting way of looking at it!"

ᴄⅣᴈ

If you want a quick and easy decision or outcome, choose a homogeneous team. If you want depth or diversity of perspectives, choose a heterogeneous team—expect a more drawn-out discussion and process, but a richer outcome.

Regardless of the definition or approach that you prefer, today's successful leaders realize that their organizations are influenced and affected by a mosaic of diverse groups—among their employees, customers, and communities. Operations in some countries have government-mandated guidelines on how diverse individuals should be accommodated. For diversity to represent a true competitive advantage, however, it is far more important for leaders to raise their self-awareness about their attitudes toward diversity and to overcome their often-unconscious biases.

One of our participants observes: "Sometimes I think we write people off because they don't fit our comfort zone of management or as a peer colleague. But if you limit your support and professional network only to people that you are comfortable with, you severely limit your own opportunity to be successful." So what can leaders do to foster a positive climate for diversity in their organizations? They need to raise awareness—and more important—be role models themselves and support champions who constantly deliver that same message. They keep it on the radar and bring it up, subtly or overtly, in meetings, on selection committees for key positions, and so forth.

Savvy leaders also understand the business case for supporting diversity:

Our CEO is very committed to the diversity of this group—we want to exceed industry standards. The organization is very results-focused and committed to pushing hard regarding diversity. High potentials in our industry are becoming more well known in the marketplace— they're being recruited. Our job is to retain and develop them.

While many leaders may be thinking, "We've done diversity," in fact, it has just reached a new plateau. We have researched the topic of diversity, concentrating primarily on women, for more than 10 years, and in that time the whole area of diversity has evolved tremendously. However, diversity champions in many organizations still concur—we still have a way to go for true equity. Of course, it's undeniable that most organizations have excellent policies on board, some of which have been mandated legislatively. And that's great. However, as some colleagues at organizations worldwide have told us: "We're not as far along as we thought we would be by now. What do you think is the problem?"

Well, it seems that we have just arrived at the next level. While the vision statement might address diversity, it's ultimately up to the managers to interpret and champion it—and quite frankly, many just don't. It's the subtle things, the intangible things. Most in the "diversity pool"—and from here on we will just say "women and minorities" for reasons of consistency— have been afforded equality at least on paper. However, we have spoken to many terrific men and women in decision-making positions for whom it just isn't on their radar when it comes to implementation and reinforcement of existing policies. But it's not intended to be exclusionary—it's generally a lack of awareness. In addition, it can take years for senior management–driven mandates actually to filter down to front-line managers and change the culture. You need a champion to keep the topic front and center on people's radar screens. The more respected and influential the person is, the better— you need highly credible people at senior levels raising visibility. One extremely well-respected woman in what was, for the most part, a totally male environment told us that she was in a meeting on how to increase diversity. In the meeting, a training film was shown on various types of subtle discrimination that goes on in organizations. As the only woman in the room, she said that all the guys were saying, "Wow, that stuff doesn't go on in *our* company." She immediately said, "Oh yeah, it does!" Because she was so well accepted as part of the team, she brought instant recognition and validation of the problem to the forefront. Twenty other less influential people could have said exactly the same thing, and no one would have paid attention—they wouldn't even have been heard. The key to getting something done about the subtle diversity issues is leveraging these champions— their credibility and voices.

As we mentioned in other chapters, you need the influential leaders on board to get things going. Although grassroots initiatives are great, it's the leaders who "get it" who implement change. They have the ability to make the policy. Interestingly enough, many women and minorities agree that, for the most part, it's not purposeful disinterest in diversity issues on the part of leaders or managers. Once again, it's just that they don't see it—it usually has never been an issue for them. But that's starting to change.

At one program on changing organizational culture, after having heard some of the diversity-related issues from men and women whom he very much respected and liked, one very senior manager said, "Okay, so maybe the next time I'm looking to choose someone for a key position, which I know will give them visibility and lead to a much higher position, I should really start looking for someone other than a white guy." It's all about raising awareness, getting the right people on board, and consistently bringing the issue up in a positive way. Younger men and women are especially driving change in many organizations. Many of these talented young leaders thrive in a diverse, global environment. The best talent believes in a meritocracy and will leave if the employer doesn't meet their expectations. They often (although not always) just see things differently regarding diversity. They have attended the same classes, they play together on sports teams, they don't see the differences in the way that their parents did, and that will enable change. Likewise, we have spoken to a number of young (white) men who have had mentors from diverse and underrepresented groups. They see them as colleagues first and not as gay or Hispanic or disabled.

As these future leaders take on higher-level positions, the culture inevitably will change and become more diverse. But it is incumbent on underrepresented groups to take a role in improving the diversity mix in their organizations' leadership as well. One senior leader gives an example for women that is equally applicable for other diverse groups:

One of our challenges for women leaders is that they often times feel very isolated at the top. Therefore, they need to develop relationships, especially with other women at their level. They need to reach out and connect with their peers. To address this, we have established a number of women's networks across the globe. Our networks provide these professional women with an opportunity to get to know one another, share experiences and ideas, and develop a broader network of colleagues and clients. The networks are both changing our culture and enhancing our bottom line.

Change is needed in the way organizations identify leaders who represent the diversity of their employees and customers. In many organizations, there continues to be a white male model for the most part. And although change is beginning to take place, the situation is similar in some business schools. However, in the current war for talent, many organizations are not developing diverse leaders to their full potential—and to the detriment of the firms, these emerging leaders are leaving as a consequence. Developing the next generation of diverse leaders is a key role for organizations worldwide.

Some interesting collaborative programs are emerging on the horizon, however. A number of well-respected organizations offer specialized leadership programs—leadership programs for women, employees of color, and so forth—in complement to traditional leadership development rather than relying on a one-solution approach. However, although 95 percent of the career and leadership issues are gender-, ethnicity-, or culture-neutral, many members of these groups will not attend what they see as "segregated" events, which, to them, may be construed as remedial. It is critical, therefore, not only that the organizational culture embrace diversity but also that individual managers are evaluated and rewarded for taking an active role in recruiting, promoting, and retaining as wide a range of diverse talent as possible. Given the long lead time to make significant changes in day-to-day attitudes, it is crucial that senior leaders act as role models in creating a more diverse management team. By creating a senior-level diversity task force or by appointing an executive-level post of chief diversity officer, senior leadership sends the message that there is a business case to be made for diversity as a key to the firm's competitive advantage. As the diversity at higher levels improves, critical mass increases for real change throughout the organization.

We have seen this many times first hand. Many men and women—peers, bosses, and subordinates—get along extremely well with virtually no evidence of race or gender differences. They just don't see it. One woman also commented on an informal conversation on this topic in which a senior man was chatting with several female colleagues, one of whom was gay. He added, "I've never seen or really focused on any differences between you and me—it has just never come up. I've always considered our professional relationship the same as between guys. However, I think that one of the reasons why guys tend to hang out together is just a comfort thing. Nothing malicious; it's just habit." While women and minority managers need more opportunities to be identified for leadership development, as one of our participants said, "It gets you in the door. The rest is up to you." But creating an environment that fosters effective communication and trust is particularly important in advancing diversity in an organization—and that's up to its leaders.

We've started to hear from some of our colleagues that their organizations are now recognizing the business imperative for diversity. They are beginning to realize that they don't reflect their market or their customers. There's a disconnect, and it's having a business impact. Some have told us that when they have gone to meetings, the customer team is widely diverse, and their companies have "mostly all white guys." Increasingly this is being called to their attention by their clients, and sometimes they don't get the business because of it.

Organizations—that is, their leaders—need to assess continually who is being selected for key positions, teams, recruitment, and promotions. They must concentrate on getting a diverse pool and bringing them to the table. One senior female executive was talking to a colleague who was telling her that there were no qualified women for a vice president position he was hiring for. She said, "If I can get you some names, would you at least take a look at them?" He said, "Sure." She gave him a list of nearly 20 outstanding women from across the organization. He did end up hiring one of them— but initially they just weren't in his sphere.

Likewise, when a former colleague was asked to help her organization identify potential areas to recruit more exceptional candidates of color in engineering, one of the first things she asked was, "Where are you currently looking for this talent?" At that point, the organization was recruiting primarily only from the top five engineering schools in the country. She said, "Okay, if there are only five minority engineering graduates a year in the schools we're considering, and approximately 20 percent of people we recruit actually end up working for us, that's one person. And every other organization is looking for the same talent. We need to recruit the top minority students at a number of schools, including historically black colleges and universities. It often just takes someone getting different people on the radar screen. As she said, "We don't want to lower our standards—we want a deeper pool—access to greater numbers of highly qualified applicants." Again, as a number of our (women and minority) colleagues have mentioned over the years, this can only get people to a point. You need to perform and get results.

DIVERSITY AND LEADERSHIP LEARNING STYLES

Our earlier books have focused on the particular issues for women in career and leadership development. However, in presenting our research findings and working with a wide spectrum of organizations, we have found that there is a great deal of commonality among the issues, challenges, and needs of women with those in other diverse groups. In fact, we have heard time and again that these concerns are not just "women's issues." What is good for women (or other minority groups) is good for all employees and can be extrapolated readily to represent diversity in all its forms.

Over the years, we have spoken to many women who are business school professors, students, or graduates about the experiences of women in business schools and beyond. The answers are generally the same—it's a necessary evil or a proving ground that is to be endured with the expectation of a payoff at the end. But why is it that, statistically, MBA programs are comprised of a mere 30 percent or so of women, whereas other professional schools have reached or exceeded 50 percent? First, many women have doubts about the perceived or actual skills needed to succeed in business school—quantitative skills, for example. In addition, most agree that there are relatively few female role models at schools and in business and that the most common teaching methods generally accommodate the learning styles of men rather than women. One of our colleagues, Dr. Anita Ferdenzi, is an expert in learning styles, and we have spoken often about this relatively new area. She says that some people learn most effectively by doing, whereas others need to relate to something visually. While some people can hear something and instantly understand it, others need continuous practice. Traditional courses of all kinds usually emphasize just one or two approaches, which may leave many learners out of the loop. A few years ago a television program on female high school students highlighted two approaches to learning in a calculus-based physics course. The first class (with only two girls in it) demonstrated a traditional learning style—each student working individually on a problem and raising his or her hand when finished. The (male) teacher wandered around the room, and when a student raised his or her hand, he said—out loud—either, "Yes, that's the correct answer," or, "No, that's not correct." The first few hands to go up—boys'—were all correct. The first girl who tentatively raised her hand was told publicly that her answer was incorrect. What a motivator! On the other hand, the experimental class, taught by the same teacher, featured an all-girls course that included team learning, information sharing, and peer mentoring, where students who got it more quickly helped their teammates. There was talking and laughing—about calculus! Many of the girls who were interviewed—some of whom initially did not want to take a girls-only class, concerned that it would be watered down—were excited with the format and achieved outstanding results. At the end, the course was so successful that the school decided to offer this course format again—for girls. The first thing that we thought was—why just for girls, probably the boys would learn better this way too? It was obvious that this learning style based on action learning, discussion, discovery, and sharing increased the learning dramatically.

The lesson here? Obviously, the predominantly male model is no longer valid in an increasingly diverse world. A number of the organizations we spoke to also were moving increasingly to this inclusive, active learning model. Several of our participants noted the 70-20-10 model; that is, 70 percent of the leadership learning time is spent on doing, 20 percent on coaching and mentoring, and just 10 percent on classroom learning. New learning style approaches must be considered and implemented, including action learning and real-world experiences, to maximize the opportunities for learning leadership among traditionally underserved students and employees.

Professor David Thomas has found that experiences and credentials communicate people's potential value as employees, which is their human capital. However, their social capital is measured by the resources available through the employee's social networks, affecting their ability to connect with others. The better or higher the status of one's credentials and connections, the more likely one is to have an advantage in competition for jobs.[1] However, many organizations are not fully realizing the potential of emerging leaders from diverse groups owing, in part, to the fact that many high potentials are identified for leadership development programs and assignments by advocates and sponsors—who frequently represent the current (and often white and male) face of their leadership. On the other hand, underrepresented talent may tend to minimize the differences in their views, values, and behaviors to "better fit" the traditional management/leadership model. For these reasons, it is often difficult for them to find mentors with whom they can build a trusting relationship or even to gain access to the traditional environments where these mentoring relationships are established. Once again, this is not a case of intentional exclusion—it is often a case of human nature in which senior managers see something of themselves in their protégés and are unconsciously drawn to them. Unless they make a conscious decision to overcome this tendency, they may overlook many highly qualified, talented potential leadership development participants.

One situation is to create an environment—and perhaps subsequent systems—to enable many individuals to gain access to diverse mentors. Likewise, it is incumbent on future leaders to create their own mentoring network (see Chapter 7).

SPECIAL-INTEREST NETWORKS

Many female and minority employees state that membership in a special-interest network at work, such as an African-American network, a women's network, a gay and lesbian network, or a Hispanic network, gives them the opportunity to talk to others going through similar experiences in different parts of the organization. This not only gives them an invaluable social network but also expands their professional network beyond their department or division. In our research, one trend that emerges frequently is that women and minorities focus on working hard but often fail to take advantage of opportunities to network as broadly as they should and may operate in a silo. One executive adds his thoughts: "Women are great when it comes to achieving results in their own groups, but many keep their heads down and don't look beyond the team. It's imperative to network outside the area you work in. That's how things get done in an organization." Especially in large organizations, it is often difficult to cultivate a network beyond one's own division or immediate circle. Therefore, networks that encompass both vertical and horizontal integration within the organization can be essential to gain a more comprehensive understanding of the organization as a whole, as well as to promote one's visibility to a larger and more diverse group—people above you and below you, internally and externally. Likewise, many of our colleagues and clients tell us that they also participate in special-interest networks outside the work environment, such as theater or book groups, volunteer opportunities, sports, and other activities to broaden their experience and opportunity to make interesting connections.

However, various leadership development options such as women-centered programs; African-American, Hispanic, and gay and lesbian networks; and other specific interest opportunities often are an excellent complement to traditional leadership development programs and another avenue to examine issues—general and specific—as well as possible strategies and solutions. They are an opportunity to discover role models, establish far-reaching networks, and meet potential mentors or sponsors. In addition, to allay the perception that sometimes arises—specifically that these courses are in some way "remedial" for people who "need help"—we recommend that some programs sponsored by diversity network groups be created to have a wide appeal to a general audience and be open to anyone who may be interested. As a result, individuals from across the organization have an opportunity to interact with each other and learn more about the specific issues for members of underrepresented groups.

These various forums also provide an opportunity to discuss issues specific to each group's particular situation. Members learn about finding their best leadership style and exploring ways in which they can add value to the organization. They may become more proactive in taking charge of their own careers by identifying potential mentors, considering options for next steps in the career path, and so forth. In these groups, we almost always use small-group exercises regardless of the size of the group or time limitations. This approach achieves several things. First, it is a less threatening opportunity for attendees to expand their networks and interact with colleagues—almost always including many whom they ordinarily may never have had the opportunity to meet. They have a setting in which to share experiences and discover commonalities and interests (both personal and professional). In addition, potential mentors are often in the group and at the tables. They provide guidance, advice, and direction to junior attendees during the session, but more important, such groups also provide more senior attendees with the chance to see how these people think, communicate, solve problems, lead, and manage teams. These sessions give the participants exposure to key people, people who are always looking for talent—especially heretofore undiscovered talent. Of course, these are also outstanding opportunities for participants to actually practice these key leadership skills. As organizations introduce policies and programs aimed at improving diversity, they greatly improve the environment for all their employees.

Another interesting example of diversity in networks is the Black Enterprise/AXA Advisors Ski Challenge. Started six years ago by Earl Graves, founder of *Black Enterprise Magazine,* now more than 700 African-American skiers and snowboarders attend the weekend event, which includes networking, social events, and financial and business seminars. The purpose of the event is to bring African-American business leaders from across the country together to meet each other and share secrets to success. However, Graves also makes a point to invite prominent white executives to facilitate high-level networking that often would not happen in a "majority" environment. The event has been so successful that it routinely sells out quickly. In addition, the company sponsors other high-visibility events, including the Black Enterprise/Microsoft Entrepreneurs Conference and the Black Enterprise/Pepsi-Cola Golf and Tennis Challenge.[2]

CHAPTER SUMMARY
Success Secret #6: Leading in a Diverse Environment

♦ Diversity allows people to see things from a different perspective, a different frame of reference. It offers a different way of analyzing a problem and offers diverse solutions.

♦ Organizations need champions, influential leaders to be consistently raising awareness on diversity, suggesting potential candidates for future leadership positions and visible teams and projects.

♦ The next generation of leaders is where real diversity will emerge—they are at school together, in early leadership positions together, and they see fewer differences.

♦ Organizations must focus on creating an environment of diversity—they need to concentrate on results, not just quotas. However, it is important not to lower standards but to create a deeper pool of potential leaders.

♦ People learn and develop in many different ways. Leadership development strategies should address a number of different learning styles, including experiential action learning.

♦ Organizations and individuals have to explore new and different ways to facilitate diverse groups to get to know each other, building trusting relationships and friendships.

Developing a Mentoring Network

ოს

*[Those] . . . who advance the furthest all share one character-
istic—a strong network of mentors and corporate sponsors
who nurture their professional development.*[1]

We have talked to a lot of leaders and future leaders over the years—
from high potentials to chief executive officers (CEOs) of major
global corporations—and one thing that most of them share is
that they have had mentors—at least one but often several. Their mentors
were sponsors, advocates, and people who saw something in them and helped
them get noticed. Traditional recipients of mentoring have generally been
the "A" players—the best 10 percent or so of managers who deliver results
and inspire others, the ones everyone wants on their team and in their firm.
Organizations do everything they can to attract them, develop them, and
keep them. This is stating the obvious. But there are relatively very few of
these superstars—and they know their worth. Their skills are highly portable
and can be lured easily by others seeking their exceptional talent. But what
about the other 90 percent? Specifically, there is the group just below these
superstars that consistently performs at a very good level and may benefit
greatly from increased mentoring. They are the hard workers who may,
given the right opportunities and guidance, advance to the A level and be
exceptional leaders in the future. And here is where the strategies in this
chapter can be applied most effectively. One executive and former general
offers this insight:

*As a military commander, I had the same issues that anyone in a
corporate environment has—finding enough qualified people to
fill my management positions. I didn't have enough majors to fill
all the vacancies I had in my division requiring this experience,*

and I didn't have many qualified captains to substitute for them. In addition, several of my battalion commanders were a bit weak. So I looked for the eight best majors I had and assigned them to command those battalions requiring more effective leadership. But this still left a gap in experienced majors for the remaining positions I had. So I filled the positions on my staff with the remaining majors and moved up the best captains I could find. This provided an opportunity for the "poorer" majors to be mentored by the really strong ones, and it also gave opportunities to cultivate the "best" captains for the future of the Army.

Mentoring is a word that is used widely but probably little understood. If you ask someone what it means, he probably will say, "It's someone, usually an older, more experienced person—often a boss—who 'shows you the ropes,' gets you noticed, and gives advice and support." But realistically, this intense, one-on-one relationship of someone looking out for your best interests is not going to happen for the average person. The best that most people can hope for is the occasional bit of advice or a "heads up" on a job opening. However, we have long advocated taking control of one's own career—identifying a number of people who, in the aggregate, can serve in a comprehensive mentoring role—not just one person, but many: a network of mentors. One of our senior participants concurs:

Some people and companies can rely too much on training per se. Emerging leaders should be proactive about their own development by finding mentors in their own and other areas, looking for cross-functional opportunities, and being willing to work hard and put in the necessary time.

First, individuals should identify what mentoring needs they have at this point in their career—a type of *mentoring needs audit.* If they were to have a cadre of people mentoring them, what would these people look like—what would be their skills, their style, and their background? Who can fulfill specific needs, where do you find them, and how do you approach them? Mentoring needs are dynamic and must be calibrated periodically—what is required at one point in a career may be dramatically different than three years ago or three years from now. Some people will identify a number of potential mentors; for others, a few will suffice. It is less about the number of potential mentors in a network and more about how well suited they are or will be to current needs. These needs will evolve and change as one gains experience, moves on to another position, takes on a new project or challenge, has a personal life change, and so forth. These "audits" should be done every few years or at particular transition periods.

What are possible mentoring roles that up-and-coming leaders may need? Perhaps they need someone who can show them the ropes and give advice, a person who can get them the information they need when they need it—on deals, on jobs, and on emerging trends. Or perhaps they need a sponsor, an advocate, or a champion—a person who can make sure that they get the right stretch assignments, global assignments, or rotations or a person who can introduce them to the right people, invite them to the right events, and give them the best opportunities. Or perhaps they need a person to make them more visible in the organization and give them legitimacy and credibility. However, one potential challenge with sponsorship is the connotation of the "in group or the out group"—that certain people will be identified automatically for sponsorship because of their type. There can be the connotation of a senior, influential, usually white man who sees a man who "reminds me of myself at that age." The sponsorship becomes a one-on-one "mini-me" type of relationship between a senior man and a more junior man who looks, acts, and thinks just like him. Some women and minorities may resist using the term *sponsor* because, in their own minds, it gives an image of the "old boys network"—and they may be right. In some cases, although the concept is interchangeable, the word *champion* may be better to use than *sponsor*. *Champion* connotes more a sense of a senior, experienced person reaching out to a number (most likely a limited number) of future leaders, perhaps still taking younger high potentials under his or her wing, but several—and diverse—people, not just one. Mentors also provide essential feedback. One leader shares his thoughts on this:

Part of mentoring is giving good feedback. Most people have a hard time being tactfully honest with others. They're concerned that they risk destroying those relationships. Many people end up just avoiding it. But it's really a lifelong exercise that you have to proactively take on.

Once the essential mentoring roles have been identified, an individual can begin to look for the right people—those with the best fit, connections, skill set, and compatible style. It can be for personal, as well as professional, development. One leader shares his experience: "I had the chance to develop early leadership experience when my boss gave me an opportunity to manage a corporate department in a discipline that was totally new for me. The experience taught me that it was my management skills that were important, and that I could transfer them to different areas within the organization and be successful, in spite of a low level of technical knowledge of the area I was assigned to manage. That was a terrific growth experience."

Likewise, the culture of the organization must be open to—and facilitate—this type of relationship. As one executive shares his thoughts about his organization: "Our culture is built around mentoring for all of our employees from their first day on the job." Leaders must take these formal and informal opportunities to identify and develop talent, especially latent talent. Leaders are always talking about finding the best people, the best talent—that there just aren't enough qualified leaders. It's relatively easy to identify the superstars at one end of the spectrum and those who are never going to be leaders at the other end, but this still leaves 50 to 60 percent of the workforce in limbo. And frankly, most leaders don't feel that they have the time to spend on identifying developing talent, although, as one participant reports, mentoring is sometimes an integral element of the organizational culture: "We expect our leaders to take individual responsibility for selecting and developing the people who will take over from them as they both rise through the organization."

Unfortunately, there are still potential leaders who can fall beneath the radar. Perhaps they haven't had the right opportunity to maximize their hidden talents, allowing them to shine. Perhaps it's a culture thing—their personality or unique style isn't 100 percent in sync with the organizational culture. Perhaps they just haven't had someone to take them under their wing and give them experiences, exposure, and challenges to light that spark. Whatever the reason, it requires both the individual and a cadre of mentors to maximize opportunities. One leader adds his thoughts:

If you find someone who seems to have potential, set high standards and push hard. Then stand back and see what happens. If they haven't had a lot of opportunities, let them step up to the plate.

Many people are unclear about the difference between a mentor and a sponsor. A sponsor (while still considered a mentor) often plays a more specific role. A sponsor frequently is a senior, influential person in one's own organization or at least industry—a person who usually works with an individual on a one-on-one basis. In addition to introducing their protégés to the right people, sponsors also make sure that the high potentials are considered for the key assignments necessary for advancement. They coach them on specific skills, as well as on general strategies and approaches. They give them the "inside track" regarding the organizational culture and "take them under their wing," giving them visibility, credibility, and legitimacy, as well as advice. A mentor, on the other hand, often encompasses a wider range of activities. Mentors can be sounding boards or support people—sharing their experiences and giving feedback and reassurance. They can provide personal, as well as professional, insights or advice. They can be a friend, a colleague, or a boss. The role can be formal or informal, at work or outside work. Mentors may offer frequent access or the occasional meeting. They also may provide critical feedback for protégés, especially at transition points—the big career decisions or the opportunity to take on a challenge in a different functional area, going from being the content expert to a leader of leaders to leading several departments, divisions, or functional areas. One executive reinforces this point: "Leaders must be prepared to actively engage in giving feedback. I believe in having a good personal feedback system, even if it's informal." A CEO gives his insights on the role of a mentor:

I'm a great advocate of mentoring. My credo is, "Don't worry about your own career; worry about others' careers." I recall a situation, after having received my law degree, where I was suddenly promoted two levels over a number of colleagues. One of the more senior team members let me know that I was "ticking off" my former peers. The advice I was given? "You're not looking back to reach out and bring these guys along. When you're in a group setting, make sure to compliment the accomplishments of your colleagues." My first reaction was, "Why should I? They've had the same opportunities as me." I did, however, take the advice and at the next meeting said, "John X did an excellent job on. . . ." I noticed that the group was instantly electrified. I realized that there was no downside to crediting the accomplishments of others. It always works to your advantage.

However, realizing that their own untapped potential may not yet be visible to leaders, it is incumbent on emerging leaders themselves to identify—and often approach—potential mentors based on their specific needs. In order to develop the critical mix of skills, knowledge, and behaviors these emerging leaders are looking for, there should be a number of people with whom they have developed ongoing key relationships. One senior leader we spoke to had a great insight, observing that

In my experience, the higher you advance (to a leadership position, senior partner, and so forth), the more visibility you need with

regard to those above you, at more senior levels. When you're being considered for stretch assignments, key positions, areas outside your realm, a lot of people have to be familiar with how you work, how you handle a crisis, and how you lead teams. At higher levels more people are involved in—and often have strong opinions about—whether or not you get promoted. For this reason, the more mentors, advocates, champions, and sponsors you have, the better off you are.

Likewise, several of our leaders underscored the importance of having more than one mentor for another reason—you might lose your key mentor. One mentor left the organization, and another wonderfully supportive mentor regrettably died. Their protégés didn't know where to go or what to do to develop a relationship with a new mentor, which invariably can take some time. They agreed that it would have been better for them to have one primary sponsor and a cadre of additional mentors in place to take up the role.

It's also enormously helpful to have a network of mentors to expose future leaders to a wider range of leadership skills, knowledge, competencies, and behaviors or style in order to assess which best fit their personality, style, and career goals. Especially in the uncertain, volatile environment of today's organizations, it can be essential to have a broader perspective with regard to one's own leadership development. An executive at Price-WaterhouseCoopers describes her network—both as a mentor and as a protégé: "I have five or six people who give me different things. I don't rely on one mentor, and taken together, I know that I can get the advice, listening and co-counseling I need when I need it. Don't get hung up on a formal definition of mentoring—make it work for you. It could be 10 minutes by phone twice a year. It could be more face-to-face time when you need it, for example, in a new role or dealing with a specific problem. Be brave, go find people who are respected, and ask them if they can help you. They may say no, but in my experience, people are pleased to be asked. I mentor around 10 to 20 people at any one time, and with each of them we contract as to what I can give, what they need, and how it will work at the start so that expectations are managed well." The CEO of a financial institution concurs: "I think the need to have a variety of mentors can't be emphasized enough. People think that one or two are sufficient. But to really develop your own management and professional identity, it is a good idea to take a little bit from as many good examples as possible."

VIRTUAL MENTORING NETWORKS

We attended a session at an American Society for Training & Development conference on mentoring presented by Dr. Belle Rose Ragins, a leading expert in the area of mentoring, in which one of the most interesting points was that of the boundaryless nature of mentoring. Dr. Ragins mentors people worldwide, usually through e-mail, and has found that effective relationships can be developed globally using technology. These far-reaching networks—some people refer to them as a "web of networks"—are increasingly effective for individuals' mentoring needs today. The rapidly changing workplace, including globalization and fast-paced technology advances, has allowed a new perspective on the mentoring process, one that does not focus on a single mentor. In addition, the days of most employees working at a single location or even primarily at "headquarters" are history. Employees are widely dispersed geographically—both nationally and internationally. People often work virtually—part time or full time—from home or while on the road. These workplace changes have made mentoring increasingly difficult. Those in sales and consulting, whose normal workweeks involve four or five days per week out of the office, have unique challenges—visibility, building informal relationships, and getting on the radar of key decision makers. Through technology, virtual mentoring networks become a very real asset. Although it cannot necessarily provide a substitute for face-to-face mentoring, the Internet has revolutionized the way we gather information and share it with others. Likewise, less expensive and more accessible telecommunications systems have dramatically changed the entire way we communicate. Global Web casts and virtual conferences are held routinely today—even for small businesses or universities. International conference calls are inexpensive and easy. However, despite the greater accessibility of mentors, emerging leaders themselves must take much of the initiative to make the contact. They have to make the effort to be noticed.

> *I really work at keeping up with my networks, my mentors—I keep in touch; I call them frequently just to say hi, to see what's going on. Last year when my formal mentor left the firm, a couple of partners called me and took me on—one is in Chicago and the other one is in New York. They said, "I know Carol has left; just give me a call." Another partner is not an official mentor but is incredibly powerful and gives me a lot of support I need. They tell me what I need to do, and I've been very proactive about their feedback. But senior partners don't just pick up the phone to call—I've been very systematic in reaching out to them.*

THE IMPORTANCE OF DIVERSITY
IN MENTORING NETWORKS

One thing that I have seen is the importance of women being able to work easily with men by developing an understanding of the differences between the genders—and also an understanding of other women who possess more masculine characteristics (i.e., leadership style), if you want to call them that. One of the roles of a mentor, for example, may be to facilitate the understanding of differences in management style and the appropriate reaction and interaction.

It is no surprise that the workplace is becoming increasingly diverse in terms of gender, race, global location, culture, and generation. Internally or externally, within a specific functional unit, or along the supply chain, individuals need to build a more diverse mentoring network. This enhanced network can provide leaders with many different perspectives on the same issue, as well as a wide range of insights and experience. Likewise, with a wider range of mentors in your network, you are exposed to many leadership styles, personalities, and approaches, enabling you to find your own best style. One young leader shares his experience:

Sometimes people mentor you—and you may not even like them as a person, but they give you great information or feedback. My former boss was not a particularly likable person. Every time I would hand him my monthly reports—which I spent many hours preparing— he would always answer, "So what? Where's the benefit, how does it impact our bottom line?" After hearing that a couple of times, I made sure that I always asked myself those questions as I was writing my reports. I worked much harder on them. I hate to admit it, but he did push me to do better work.

Another thing that we hear from our clients and colleagues is that they are increasingly aware of the need to reflect their customers, clients, and supply chain—they need to have diversity on their teams. One recounted a story of going out to a customer with "all white guys with gray hair" on the team, whereas their customer's team consisted of "two women, one Hispanic guy, one African-American guy, and one white guy. We didn't get the business."

Although not everyone's senior leadership is on the diversity bandwagon, there is still a lot that people can do to gain visibility, credibility, and sponsorship. For one thing—and many of our leaders, both men and women, have said the same thing—it's critical to identify the senior people who "get it"—forget about the others for now. We have worked with many organizations that have addressed this issue, and they often are surprised at how many advocates there are, even in rather "diversity unfriendly" organizations. If you haven't read Chapter 3 on knowledge networks, take a look. We're talking about tacit knowledge here—finding out through the underground network who the people are who "get it"—and getting them on your contact list.

MAKING YOUR MENTORS LOOK GOOD

It's a good idea to develop a portfolio of mentors in your mentoring relationships, different ones for different needs. You will talk to some frequently; others, just occasionally. But it's the same as a professional portfolio of skills, competencies, and knowledge. You need a wide range, as well as a specific focus. However, one interesting point here is that a number of leaders that we have spoken to over the years have mentioned that many young leaders often lack "soft skills" that are critical in building these relationships: communication, interpersonal relations, emotional intelligence, and initiative. One senior executive adds: "I don't want to have to chase after people in our high-potentials group to get things done—I want the people who will come to me with ideas, challenges, or solutions because they've been thinking about it all night. I want people who have an enthusiastic attitude and passion, but also the confidence to make things happen."

Another leader gave advice to future leaders, saying that not only is it essential to be proactive in seeking out a number of mentors but also that it's important to be a good protégé as well. She recommends being a self-starter—do more than is expected, exceed your mentor's expectations. These leaders have put themselves out there to sponsor future leaders, and it's critical to prove to them—and others—that you are worthy of the investment. If you screw up, your mentor's reputation is on the line. She adds that these relationships usually develop over time and that they have to be nurtured. A protégé's success reflects positively on the mentor—it highlights her good instincts in making an excellent choice of taking that person on. Conversely, if protégés don't hold up their end to perform above expectation, this can reflect badly on their mentors. The entire responsibility of the protégé's success in a mentoring relationship does not rest solely with the mentor. Another leader concurs:

I've been given a number of promotions in my career that were a stretch, but my bosses always stayed involved to support me. They didn't want me to fail, not only for my sake, but for their own as well. This mutual trust allows both the young leader and the sponsor to feel comfortable in testing leadership skills in slightly riskier opportunities.

Despite their level of achievement, even the most senior leaders need mentoring, either formal or informal. It's a continuous learning process—building new skills and competencies and gaining feedback and advice, which is especially important in turbulent times. One CEO adds his thoughts: "I currently coach a 34-year-old female CEO for about two hours every couple of weeks. We talk about all kinds of things that she will need, such as running board meetings, dealing with the press, and so forth. It's a mutually positive relationship, and I believe that she would add that I have increased her productivity." When we asked this CEO how he came to mentor this woman, he said that a colleague introduced them and thought that it would be a good match and that his skills would complement her experiences. (The informal underground network at work!) Many of the leaders we spoke to underscored the importance of their own networks. While they may not specifically consider them as such, the mentoring roles that members of the leaders' networks play, even unconsciously, may include giving advice on a turnaround or acquisition process and sharing their insights on dealing with specific issues, such as developing a new global market presence, or undertaking a major culture change. There are CEO summits and many other resources for the highest-level executives. The context may be different, but the process is the same—a pool of smart, talented, experienced people who can offer advice, guidance, information, and support.

LEADER INVOLVEMENT IN DEVELOPING NEXT-GENERATION LEADERS

One theme we heard from many of our participants was the importance of experienced leaders being involved in the development of future leaders. In the past, most leadership development was seen as a human resources (HR) initiative: training courses and the like. But now, the most forward-thinking companies in terms of developing and mentoring future leaders agree— senior managers must be involved. In many cases the CEOs have spearheaded the movement, working closely with their teams and even spending significant time with the future leaders themselves. Many organizations agree that this time is invaluable in determining bench strength in order to gauge the future success of their vision and strategies. One participant shared his thoughts on the involvement of leaders in mentoring and development:

A critical component of mentoring and developing leaders is the involvement of the senior staff. For example, as a part of a rigorous offsite session for high-potential managers, each participant meets with two managing directors for face-to-face feedback on strengths and improvement needs, based on the results of aptitude tests, oral presentations, role-playing, and observation over nearly three days. Our participants have received this candid feedback very well, and it's clear that, as a result of the extensive follow-up and customized development plans, they are far better leaders having had the experience. The event also allows our most senior leaders to become familiar with many high-potential managers.

CHAPTER SUMMARY

Success Secret #7: Developing a Mentoring Network

♦ Only approximately 10 percent of employees are the superstars, the A players. However, the group just below these superstars that consistently performs at a very good level may be well served by increased mentoring. These hard workers may, given the right opportunities and guidance, advance to the A level and be exceptional leaders in the future.

♦ Individuals should identify what mentoring needs they have at a point in their career—a mentoring needs audit. They should seek out a cadre of people to mentor them based on compatible style, background, and ability to advance their career.

♦ It is important to mentor others, as well as seek out mentoring for one's own career.

♦ As protégés seek out mentors, they should be aware of the risks that their mentors have taken to identify them as someone with potential—they have put their reputations on the line. It is essential that the protégés live up to their potential and do an outstanding job in that role.

♦ Mentoring networks do not happen by chance. They require consistent maintenance—keeping in touch and calling to say hello—not only when you need something but also keeping mentors updated, doing things for them, and being available to help them. It's not a one-way street.

- Seek out diversity in mentoring networks—different perspectives, different ways of thinking, and different experiences, as well as differences in race, culture, geographic location, generation, and so on.

- Mentoring is a learning experience. It is important to learn from mistakes and use the lessons learned and mentor feedback for future situations.

- Leaders, as well as future leaders, need mentoring, advice, and coaching—it's just at a different level. It may include advice on a turnaround, best practices on a culture change, coaching on the development of a global presence, and so forth.

Expanding Your Global Focus

⌒⌒

International experience is very important, since many of our clients are global. We want people who are change champions, the best people who can think strategically and who ask the right questions, such as, "What do we need to do differently in this environment?"

Several trends have brought greater attention to the need for globalization in recent years: hypercompetition on a global scale—bringing with it both the challenge of new competitive threats and the opportunity for organic growth as companies expand into new markets worldwide; innovations in technology, communications, and logistics that make it easier to move information and products around the world; changes in social and economic conditions that have increased demand worldwide for both mainstream and niche brands; and an increasingly international makeup of senior management teams who have a global perspective as their frame of reference.

Developing competitive global managers is a strategic issue for many firms. Since these companies are creating and implementing far-reaching global strategies to reach new customer and employee pools, the preparation and advancement of qualified senior managers and high-potential employees are viewed as major factors in the success or failure of these increasingly global businesses. One of our participants articulates a recurring theme among senior leaders:

We are fundamentally changing—we are redefining what business we are in. The skill set has to change to reflect this new environment. Global expansion is responsible for much of our new growth— growing global leaders is key for us. And we have to look beyond just our expat leaders and grow local leaders as well.

There has been growing concern in corporate and other organizational circles that not only is there a critical shortage of qualified leaders in the pipeline but also more specifically a desperate shortage of individuals with leadership experience or potential *plus* global experience. As one executive we spoke to said:

> *It's been talked about for a long time, but for many of us, there's not enough growth left in the U.S. We're a much more mature market for many goods and services. Top-line growth has to come from abroad. And there's an intense worldwide increase in interest in the same few people with leadership skills and global perspective. It used to be that we were competing with those in our industry, but now I'm getting calls from people in totally different industries trying to see if I know anyone for top-level global jobs. Everyone has to be more creative in the way they approach this problem. It's not going to go away. And I'm not necessarily talking about leaders who have spent time as expats or world travelers, but rather those with a truly global perspective. It's a global economy now. One of our greatest challenges is dealing in a global context—about 75 percent of our business in non-U.S.-focused.*

In the twenty-first century, the global economy is no longer just the flow of goods but is increasingly the "flow of capital, people, and information."[1] Technology, among other things, has expedited the flow, diminishing barriers. The Internet, computer networks, instant messaging, video teleconferencing, and so forth have created a 24/7 environment with its own challenges. However, even more critical for organizations worldwide is finding the talent to lead in this increasingly global environment. As one participant shares, "We leverage technology to bring together global teams—to create a truly global climate."

For many people, *global* may mean simply an organization with a national home base, let's say in the United States, but with customers in other regions of the world. For others, it may include international offices or production facilities in addition to its headquarters in the home country, or to some it is an organization with a home country but significant divisions or businesses located elsewhere in the world. However, truly global companies have remarkably little identity with regard to a specific country—or even region. We were speaking to one executive recently about this differentiation, and he added, "Most companies think that they're global, but they're really not. HSBC is one of the few I could really assign that description to—a truly global company."

HSBC has developed a consistent corporate identity owing in part to the way that it develops its senior management team. People can't get to a senior position unless they have worked in more than one market—and indeed, most of them have worked in at least two or three. Living and working in different countries broadens the mind; it allows you to see things from a different perspective. Such companies are always looking for well-rounded individuals not so much for their backgrounds with respect to what or where they have studied but rather for their cultural sensitivity and readiness to be open-minded, as well as their drive and initiative. The management team seeks individuals who can lead effectively in a global environment with highly diverse communities.[2] HSBC's recruitment strategies have become far more global in their reach because the company now recruits at more than 60 universities worldwide—a situation that is quite different from 20 years ago, when leaders came primarily from British institutions. This global perspective regarding recruitment not only allows the organization to become far more representative of their clients—and responsive to their needs—but also allows for greater understanding and collaboration among their employees. As HSBC Chief Executive Officer (CEO) Stephen Green adds, "It would be a far less interesting, creative—and fun—place if we lost that richness of diversity that is so valued here."

Organizations seeking global talent focus on getting the right skills and the right attitude in their recruits. People with the "right education" and foreign language skills don't necessarily possess the cultural sensitivity and openness to other perspectives and the ability to develop global relationships. It is important to also consider those with limited language skills or global experience who nonetheless have great passion and curiosity about the world and can work effectively in different cultures. These attributes are at the center of a global attitude. This may necessitate rethinking performance expectations to measure how well employees demonstrate open-mindedness, collaboration across the organization, and shared accountability.

One global executive shares that it is critical to understand and manage authority relationships. In Asia, for example, staff members hesitate to question or contradict their manager in a group for fear of losing face. Leaders, therefore, have to work hard to build credibility with the local team and to make sure that the rationale for choosing a particular course of action and the goals for achieving it have been clearly communicated to gain their team's buy-in. The group also needs to know that you understand local and regional issues and that they are integrated into the big picture.

Leaders have to be able to bring cultures together. They must be able to effectively identify and develop people with global attitudes. And they should be personally involved in developing talent at all levels of the organization—

from senior management to sales reps in the field to front-line personnel—by personally talking to their people, listening, and observing. Although admittedly time-consuming, this deep involvement, vertically and horizontally, allows senior leadership to be on the pulse point of issues, challenges, market trends, and client needs. Avon CEO Andrea Jung takes this type of personal approach to identifying and nurturing global talent, keeping an eye on emerging talent even several levels below her. Her management team is evaluated not only on how members select new managers but also on how they develop them to contribute to the global community. This has been extremely effective in developing a truly global business culture, which includes significant sales outside North America.[3]

THE CHANGING WORLD OF GLOBAL LEADERSHIP

Smart people are in demand everywhere for reasons beyond an aging workforce and the demographic talent shortage. The All India Management Association predicts that by 2020 there will be a dramatic universal shortage of smart workers.[4] A 2003 National Association of Manufacturers report states that "a skilled-worker gap will start to form in 2005, widening to 5.3 million workers by 2010 and 14 million by 2020. The labor shortages that plagued high-tech companies in the halcyon days of 1999 and 2000 will look like a minor irritation in comparison. . . . "[5] One leader we interviewed concurs: "In the old days we were competing with the other pharmaceutical companies for talent, especially in science and engineering. Now, we're competing with many different industries for the same talent. We have to make it really attractive for them to work for us." As professionals are increasingly being educated to common world standards, especially in engineering, technology, and other fields, the Internet also makes it easier to recruit them on a worldwide basis, so the global talent pool is dispersing. Increasingly, organizations worldwide must be able to identify the best global leaders, develop them, and give them incentives to stay.

Both countries and organizations, faced with the great mobility of this global workforce, increasingly must develop their own talent—they need to create more smart people. As a result, enhancing creativity and human/knowledge capital should be a significant concern for organizations worldwide. One solution is to look to their training grounds: colleges and universities. There is emerging evidence of a gap between what our organizations need—specifically the skills, knowledge, competencies, and behaviors of future leaders, and the preparation academic institutions are providing—especially in business schools. Partnerships between institutions of higher learning and organizations (their end users) are essential to prepare future leaders for a more global focus and to identify needs, gaps, and solutions to this global problem. An academic leader shares: "We look for those who display sensitivity to diversity and globalization—those who can bring out the best in others in a new and different world." These initiatives can run the gamut from training high-level Ph.D.s and MBAs to career education programs focusing on technology and other key areas. European universities have increased the number of international students significantly owing to the global focus of their MBA programs, for example, as opposed to universities in the United States, which have been slower to adapt. These global perspectives undoubtedly better prepare students for future leadership positions.

In countries such as China and India, for example, long sources of math, science, and technology talent, economies have now grown to a point where they can offer their own high-potential individuals real opportunities for education and jobs without having to go abroad. Likewise, countries including Australia, Finland, and Canada, among others, have invested substantially in higher education and are beginning to emerge as creative leaders. Some experts believe that since young, talented people tend to remain where they are educated, the centers of innovation may begin to shift to these emerging creative centers. The economic stakes are potentially enormous. New Zealand and Ireland, for example, have seen phenomenal growth in what some call the "creative class," whose members are coming up with the next great ideas, designing innovative new products, writing the cutting-edge software, and working on breakthrough medical research.[6] Similar collaborations among corporate, academic, and government partners are thriving in Brazil, Taiwan, Korea, Malaysia, and other areas.

It is no surprise that for an increasing number of organizations worldwide, including those involved in financial services, technology, law, and consulting, intellectual capital is fast becoming a commodity. Such skills as complex problem solving, analytical skills, the ability to connect seemingly unrelated things, and seeing the "big picture" are highly sought after. Their knowledge workers are what differentiate these organizations. Some leaders believe that "where talent goes, innovations and economic growth follow." In this increasingly global economy, as the competition for smart, talented people grows exponentially, the countries that do the most to attract—and retain—the best and the brightest stand to gain the greatest increases in that growth.[7]

Many organizations are developing truly global strategies rather than country-by-country approaches that integrate business across geographic boundaries.[8] Increasingly, leaders need to think along this line—not just what's going to be profitable for your business unit but also company-wide and worldwide. The future success of your plans for the U.K. market, for example, cannot be at the expense of the Latin American market. As a result, some organizations are beginning to do full-scale global launches for new products rather than using a cascading product launch that starts in one geographic region to give time to "see what happens." While established companies often undergo a significant culture change to accommodate the global perspective, newer companies, having "grown up" in this environment, often have the luxury of being "born global." Technology companies, for example, often are more global in scope because they are not constrained by physical borders.

However, Internet-based products and services are not the only ones to have discovered global demand. Companies such as FedEx increasingly have promoted their ability to be consistent across global markets, emphasizing their world-standard reliability and service. Banks such as UBS and Deutsche Bank have underscored their global reach, delivering consistent, high-quality products and service across borders. At the other end of the spectrum are more unexpected applications of a world standard: modular homes being manufactured in the United States and delivered—in parts—worldwide. Companies undoubtedly less known for their global focus, such as World Homes in Florida, Horton Homes in Georgia, and Southern Energy Homes in Alabama, have discovered that using a patented global-standard frame for their modular buildings can lower shipping costs for their products significantly. Consequently, these companies have experienced great success in exporting their products—in this case, entire modular buildings—worldwide: a prefabricated health care facility in Russia, resort accommodations at a Beijing golf course, and single-family homes in Angola, Guam, and Lithuania. Often working with local architects and builders, many of these new global companies also customize their products to suit local tastes and building codes.[9]

Regardless of their size, product line, or service, companies seeking to expand into global markets require a globally focused customer service mind-set. A senior executive shared some advice for leaders whose organizations are involved in initiating or expanding their firm's global position:

Leaders should instill in their workforce the realization that they are now operating in all time zones, including ones where their working day and their customers' do not even overlap—so, for example, not replying immediately to an urgent customer request means a full working day is lost. Customer service has to extend beyond local office hours! In addition, different cultures and local attitudes often require greater patience and empathy—global customers can be more demanding than those in the domestic markets. And be aware of differences in cycles—don't try to force short-term returns in a culture that is based on looking at the long term. Overall, you can't really go wrong if you focus on creating a relationship built on mutual trust.

GLOBAL TEAMS/VIRTUAL TEAMS

Global teams will be used increasingly to address market opportunities that include greater competition from new and unexpected sources worldwide. Former partners along the supply chain may now create new products and services. Leaders operating in these environments increasingly will need to be on the pulse point of their global customers, understanding their needs, trends, and new markets.

Competitive advantage will be gained through alliances. Leaders must understand the implications for their industry and redefine their approach accordingly. Likewise, collaboration with smaller companies gives large companies access to innovation, and it also gives smaller companies the advantage of greater size, such as market presence and purchasing power.[10]

Among the issues that our participants raised when dealing with global teams was the need for leaders to be even-handed in their treatment of team members—be careful not to show any bias or unfairness in handing out assignments, feedback, rewards, and so forth. And particularly in an organizational setup that includes a world headquarters and remote offices, it is important for those in "outpost" sites to know that they have a champion at the home office. In addition, keep cultural diversity in mind. In some cultures, such as in the United States, competition among team members is often encouraged—star performers are praised. In other cultures, the performance and success of the team is more highly valued than that of the individual. Likewise, building effective teamwork in a global environment is a challenge to any organization. What people may think is good teamwork or leadership in one country or region may fail miserably in another owing to the cultural context. Likewise, assumptions and definitions of such things as power, hierarchies, trust, and ethics can vary widely from country to country or region to region. Unfortunately, with the shortage of globally aware leaders, the opportunities for misunderstanding, conflict, frustration, and even loss of business can be significant given this lack of preparation and understanding of other cultures.

Several of our leaders talked about global summits, both internal and external. They underscored that it is essential to get people together and talking—and as a result, they believed that the outcomes of these summits were significantly improved communication, understanding, and buy-in to initiatives. They suggested that leaders should be open about transferring best practices in one region to other global operations and markets—be aware of what can make the entire operation more efficient, effective, and profitable. One leader added that the best part of a recent emerging global leaders program was networking. Participants felt that this opportunity to get together greatly enhanced strategic global discussions and innovative solutions to challenges.

With operations in over 100 countries, we have to ensure that there is a strong connection among people in many operations to deliver a unified suite of products worldwide.

cho

We have traditionally been somewhat internally focused but have realized that we will increasingly need to take a more collaborative approach to include those inside and outside the company—and certainly on a global scale.

One aspect of building global teams mentioned by our participants is the importance of building strong relationships. Developing initial relationships is key, resulting in greater trust and communication. Although obviously more difficult, the most effective teams begin face to face, at least initially, to foster the opportunity for informal, spontaneous conversations and gathering together—finding things in common often allows members to work more collaboratively.[11] Many senior leaders we spoke to said that they took advantage of opportunities while wandering down the hall, waiting for an elevator, or dining in the lunch room to catch up with colleagues, to share information or solutions to similar issues or problems, to engage in mentoring, to offer advice, and to create informal information networks. If face-to-face meetings are not possible, we also have worked with clients on networking resource sheets, essentially capturing all kinds of information, both personal and professional, that employees and team members wish to share with colleagues. Such sheets could be posted on specific organizational Web pages with photographs and other information employees would like to share. As employees need or are interested in specific information or would like to contact others in the organization with similar issues or interests, this information can be accessed. One of our leaders mentioned that her organization is developing a global "virtual water cooler," an informal site on which employees can chat about the personal things that people working in the same location do.

The operations department of one financial giant has arranged for a flex-time situation that offers comp time and accommodates participants' schedules in their weekly conference call among their U.S., U.K, and Asian offices. If team members in various time zones have to work well beyond their normal work hours, it is compensated for the next day with options to come in late, leave early, and so forth. Team members agree that these regularly scheduled meetings work well to establish a team routine and camaraderie.

It's also important for leaders not to make assumptions about their employees' views on travel and relocation issues. By using various technologies, it is possible for some global team members to be able to remain in their home offices. Several of our colleagues have mentioned that even in this age of technology, many members of their teams still feel that they have to jump on a plane to rush to a client meeting at the drop of a hat or spend weekends away from family. With our increasingly 24/7 on-call environment, some key team members are offering diverse opinions. They're beginning to say, "Wait, I have no problem going to London for a meeting, but is there a better way than the way it's always been done?" By complementing face-to-face time with virtual options, smart thinking has dual benefits of cost savings for the firm and greatly increased employee satisfaction. One executive whose company is just about to go through a merger with a larger global organization (whose employees regularly commute worldwide) added, "The first thing I'm going to do is set up a totally state-of-the-art teleconference system." Leaders may need to think differently. Instead of relocating, will some employees be equally effective if they prefer long-distance commutes or spending one week a month at the new location? Get feedback on their needs. Communication is key.

TRANSLATING GLOBALLY

Many of our leaders emphasized the importance of developing or increasing their global presence—nearly everyone said that global issues are paramount for their future. They said that they, as organizations, had to think proactively about global teams. Everything has to translate culturally. They must focus on leveraging their resources—using the people in their organizations, as well as external resources. There are too many possibilities for miscommunication and misinterpretation about languages, culture, values, concepts of task completion, what constitutes ethical behavior, decision making, authority, conflict, and so on—don't leave it to chance. They also underscore the importance of organizations accommodating local markets and customs by understanding and leveraging the diversity of their employees and customers. They are aware of valuing local ways of doing business. Likewise, they are striving to develop partnerships with both local and global service organizations to address social causes, which can facilitate relationships that not only enable change but also build a positive presence for their organizations. The issue of balancing the sense of organizational consistency on a global scale with issues in cultural diversity is one of the major reasons why many executive teams have found it more difficult to actually implement global strategies than to develop them. Leaders should weigh the importance of structure, global brand identity, and efficiency with the flexibility necessary to respond appropriately to a wide range of employee, customer, and community needs and expectations.

For organizations that traditionally have felt that they are at the epicenter of their industries and are now transitioning to global firms, one of our participants warns that they face a huge cultural "wakeup call and challenge." He urges companies to grow or import the global talent necessary to guide them forward and avoid costly mistakes. Whatever the negative consequences of poor decisions in the domestic market have been, they will be far more expensive in a global setting in terms of time and resources needed to reverse any mistakes.

Have most organizations addressed possible issues of cross-cultural conflict? For example, key elements of Western leadership include a comfort level with conflict and acceptance of a strong individual leader calling the shots—albeit with input from the team. How does this compare, for example, with a leadership perspective in Asia, where a strong hierarchical structure based on family, respect, long-standing relationships, and in some cases, consensus is how business is done? Global awareness that relates to more than just business issues should be developed before an organization just decides to "go global."

CHAPTER SUMMARY
Success Secret #8: Exploring Your Global Focus

♦ There is a critical shortage of individuals with leadership experience or potential and global experience. Organizations worldwide need to be more creative in solving this problem.

♦ Leaders should be able not only to understand both the overt and subtle differences in culture across borders but also to bring people together on a global basis.

- The face of global leadership is changing. Whereas until recently the United States generally was the center of education and innovation, other countries are developing excellent university and corporate infrastructures and enabling greater creativity and innovation.
- Organizations increasingly are seeking a global standard, from technology to engineering, from logistics to modular home building.
- Leaders must understand the implications of "going global," including global teams, logistics, culture, and style.

Building and Leading
High-Performance Teams

☙

There are a lot of really smart people out there with great skills, a lot of knowledge. But they don't have what it takes to lead others. I'm looking for people with heart who can gather a group together and inspire them to achieve great things. Most of our people are intellectually outstanding. But if there's a choice between the person with just the 150-plus IQ or a person with the 140 IQ—but who has the passion—I'd rather have the person with passion any day.

This chapter is not about the nuts and bolts of leading a team—there's a lot of great information out there on the "how to" part—setting goals, defining roles and responsibilities, and measuring performance against your target. This chapter is largely about the intangible stuff—your instincts, thinking not only about who should be on the team but also about why, inspiring your team, looking at the "big picture," building relationships, and enabling collaboration both internally and externally. There are a lot of smart people out there who want to be noticed, valued, and given real-world experiences. They want to lead with passion. The real trick is finding them and leveraging their talents.

LEADING IN A KNOWLEDGE-BASED ENVIRONMENT
In a knowledge-based world, you have a lot of very motivated, very smart, and very capable people. However, as any seasoned leader can tell you, you're always dealing with countless variables when you're trying to pull

them together in a high-performance team. You're looking for the technical skills, competencies, and knowledge—that's a given. But there is so much more than that. You need to get the right fit, the right culture, and the right chemistry—the "karma." A lot of this is based on the intangibles—how they think, how they connect, their drive, their energy, and their commitment to coming to the best solution, not just "getting it done." One leader added these thoughts on looking at the intangibles of building a team:

What's wrong with looking at the "fuzzy stuff"—going with your instincts when you're bringing people onto teams? Nine times out of ten, that turns out to be the most important stuff anyway: how they fit, how they think, how you work together, their values.

In our interviews, a number of leaders shared their ideas about what they look for in their own team members. Of course, many of their responses shouldn't surprise you. Most leaders are looking for people who are performance-focused, results-driven, able to deliver (are actually able do the job), willing to do the job, a good fit for the position, action-oriented, have intellectual horsepower and experience, and are good decision makers. But other traits came out as well. Leaders want people on their teams who are adaptable; are good listeners; have self-confidence, agility, and a good attitude; and have commitment, a strong work ethic, and integrity. They want people who can think differently and who have the courage to raise the tough questions and disagree with senior leaders.

One senior leader added his thoughts on how he chooses individuals for top teams:

The "rulebook" advises that when recruiting senior people, you should make the process as scientific and objective as possible. Various tools such as psychometric tests have become more prevalent in recent years to reduce the risk of making the wrong selection. The hidden, or maybe not so hidden, message behind this is that if you rely in any way on your gut instinct or take into consideration the personal chemistry created (or not created) with the candidate, then you are being "sloppy" or unprofessional, given that recruiting the wrong candidate and then having to admit the mistake, fire the person, and go through the whole selection process again is an expensive, time-consuming, and often disruptive process. However, in my experience, a combination of an objective methodology for screening and assessing, in addition to the gut instinct, works well—and works better the higher up in the organization you're recruiting for.

I have always used a method of selecting five or six key attributes or requirements for the job and assessed prescreened candidates by scoring them out of a possible 10 for each one, then see who comes out on top. Time and thought spent on defining these five or six key attributes is time well spent. Obviously, the lower the level of recruitment, the more these attributes will focus on specific skill sets. Recruiting for the top team assumes the skill sets are mostly in place and you are looking more for generalist skills, as your context is different. It's more about what insights and experience the candidate can bring to the company and what they contribute to the strategy going forward. It is important to determine what specific evidence from their past track record reflects that they will drive their department, function, or operation forward in the way you envisage. Do they seem to have the intellect, the passion, the enthusiasm, and the mind-set to query, challenge, and contribute? Will they come up with insightful contributions on a regular, consistent basis and not just have the occasional flash of brilliance? Are they results-driven, and does the evidence support this? That is a mandatory requirement when recruiting for the top team.

Finally, will they fit into the team and the current culture, or be the type of personality that will help shape the culture you hope to create, if that is part of the plan? And will you personally click and get along with them? That doesn't mean that there will never be tension, conflict, or disagreement, but the power of teamwork should never be underestimated. The fundamentals of great teamwork require a group of people that click together and can work for, and with, each other almost instinctively. As someone once pointed out: "If there is something you don't like about someone during a two-hour interview, then you are going to like it a whole lot less after you have employed them and they are working for you!"

We have been talking about the importance of the team leaders and members who everyone wants on their team or leading their team—the ones "you just can just tell are going to be fantastic." However, we heard more than a few times that high-performance teams are not made up only of those "superstars." Others can offer critical elements to the team, but more behind the scenes. These are the smart, steady, hard workers that are essential to every organization and critical for every team. The ones you can depend on and you have rapport with. You know they're going to get the work done—and far more. They're low maintenance, and they serve as your confidante, your barometer of how things are going. Every team needs at least one. Without such people, the team doesn't function. One senior leader shares her thoughts:

Starting a team from scratch, I identify which members will work together well based on their skills and their alignment or fit with the organization, team, division, or department, rather than simply relying on their job title. I look for someone I can count on. Someone who is aligned with the common goal of the team—they know the goal, they're in sync with the goal. My job as team leader is to always keep everyone focused on what the goal is. It's constant reinforcement, reminding them, keeping them on target. I also have to be aware that you can't always hand pick your ideal team—there are often political reasons, like in a merger or acquisition, you have to be well represented by both companies. You may not know a lot of the players from the other company, so you don't know how they think or act. Some members are higher maintenance. Others will simply never deliver—they're just not capable. I usually look for someone who can "pinch hit," who's willing to take ownership of some of the issues. One of my usual choices is John—in addition to his innate intelligence and clear, calm way of looking at things, I find that I frequently turn to him to get a second opinion on the pulse point of the team, to gauge how things are going. He's my right-hand guy.

Another executive makes it a point to try to meet individually with the team members before they start the project to get a sense of their strengths, weaknesses, and interests. In this way, he can help to head off personality or performance problems that otherwise may blindside him down the road. He adds: "You've got to remember, a team is made up of individual members— all of whom want to feel valued and able to contribute. But also, certain personalities sometimes just don't work together. I've had people who are control freaks and can't deal with constantly ongoing issues—they need closure. Or others who think that they're doing more than everyone else— if I don't address issues to their specific satisfaction, they get upset. I confess, sometimes I've just been too busy to constantly hand hold them. But looking back, had I addressed their concerns at the time, it probably would have been easier in the long run."

In this environment of an accelerating rate of change, uncertainty, volatility, and risk, invariably there are going to be crises that need to be managed, personalities that need to be handled, and many long hours spent together. It is important to have someone on the team with the steady hand—

the voice of calm—that ensures that everything will get done and that the results will be great. One leader concurs:

We operate in a very uncertain and complex environment, so leaders have to show calm in chaos. They have to rally the troops, have passion. They have to engage people on their team to perform at their best in these conditions. But business is not war; it's creating value.

THE COLLECTIVE GENIUS OF TEAMS

Part of a leader's role is locating, attracting, assessing, and developing talent, but increasingly, it's not only about individuals—it's also about how they work together collectively. As one of our participants said: "Leaders should have a profound understanding of what it means to lead others. There's no single hero or heroine. In today's environment, the ability to lead collective change is what's important." Leaders should be thinking about leveraging those with talent into a "collective genius." What chemistry is needed among members to sustain these intense, long-term relationships? What about their technical expertise, their personal qualities, and their cultural fit? Leaders must go beyond just the obvious skills. They need to assess the viability of team members and enable them to develop, keeping in mind that individuals other than the most visible leaders also may have a significant role. While it's often easier to just get together the "usual suspects"—the people who are on every team—a number of our leaders added that they look at context, carefully considering potential team members based on what the team needs, not just titles. Think about the best teams you ever worked with—what made them great projects, assignments, or task forces? Was it a good match of talent, personalities, work ethic, style, or intellectual horsepower? A good fit? Fun? People were probably just in sync, and you could almost sense what the others needed. When one or several people left, was it just not the same? You can't put your finger on why; it just wasn't. There are many parts of a diverse team—eliminate certain individuals from the team, and it may cease to function as creatively, as effectively. In addition to task and context, you have to think about the chemistry that is needed in teams—the intangibles.

Many of our leaders said that they look for people who are agile, who can think differently, and who can learn. Those in an environment of "collective genius" know how to maintain their independence, along with collaboration. As one participant mentioned: "I'm looking for three things in leaders, first, change agility: These people can manage conflict and have the risk tolerance to deal with change. They have courage, confidence, and a demonstrated track record. Second, they need learning agility: They were solid in their last job; now they're at the next level or in other parts of the organization. They must be able to learn quickly and get results. Finally, interpersonal agility: They have to work with others to get results. They need to delegate, influence, build trust and confidence—or rebuild confidence. Individual contributors don't necessarily know how to get things done through others."

A number of our leaders stated that they also look for people with the courage to stand up and say, "Wait, I don't agree with this"—and be able to defend the reasons why. You need a diverse team in terms not only of gender, race, generation, or culture but also of different perspectives, different experiences, and from different regions. However, don't assume that this is always going to be easy—not everyone is going to thrive in such an environment. It can be fast-paced, volatile, and contentious and can take a lot more effort to get to a good result. "It takes time and energy to work with those who are different, to integrate them into the collective."[1] One of our participants concurs:

> *I think a skill I have found useful is the ability to recognize talents in people, no matter how I might feel interpersonally toward a person. This means sometimes expanding my comfort zone to work with people who at times have been difficult. This does not mean compromising myself or my values or sense of self. But it does mean I examine why a particular person seems difficult for me to work with. Upon reflection, I usually find it is just my personal bias in regard to a particular personality trait. I find some people are too direct, some people are too task-focused, or whatever. But then I realize that that is just the way they are, and it is really I who have the problem with that. If I can work with that part of his or her personality, I realize the person is actually quite talented and adds a lot of value.*

Among the responses of our participants, we increasingly saw a trend of bringing people together in teams across functions, even across industries. A number of our participants told us that it brings a completely new perspective to the solutions for enterprise-wide challenges. However, in terms of culture and logistics, it also requires a new way of looking at things, an understanding of a broader range of issues—and, of course, a far greater sense of who is in the organization, that is, more far-reaching relationships. One leader shared her thoughts:

> *Our new programs focus on applying all our resources from every department to solve a common problem. Senior leaders from every organizational unit work together to rewrite the paradigm*

for our field—we now view our challenges from a universal perspective, rather than from individual silos. We collectively take ownership of delivering cost-effective, quality programs for all our clients. As a result, we can now understand how much is spent on each critical issue and can prioritize our programs by their return on investment. Support for programs should be driven by our strategic vision—not by the budget process. But we need to "brand" our new paradigm to make it systemic for the future.

This type of collective team culture also can be difficult for those who have been recognized traditionally only for outstanding individual performance but have not necessarily embraced the importance of working in a team. A leader in global banking underscores the importance of collective genius:

Here the concept of teamwork is huge; it's a different concept from many other companies. How? We deliberately don't have a "star" system—we're almost the other extreme. It's "we," not "I." Individual performance is a given. We expect that the organization understands your contribution. It's the thinking that if two heads are better than one, ten heads are better than two. We're looking for better engagement, greater consensus building. People coming in from other cultures sometimes find this concept of team performance versus individual performance different or even difficult. However, extremes at either end—individual or team—aren't good.

MOTIVATING YOUR TEAM IN A KNOWLEDGE ENVIRONMENT

When you're working with smart, motivated people, it's not only about the tangible rewards—team success (and personal achievement) also can be strong team motivators. One leader we spoke to has a philosophy about what motivates many teams in today's organizations and how they should be rewarded:

Although everybody likes money, they aren't necessarily motivated by cash, trips, toys, and trinkets. They want the recognition that at least once in their life they made a difference and contributed to a world-class effort—their equivalent of a gold medal.

Using an example from the pharmaceutical industry, this leader advocates providing an opportunity to rise through the organization, with the associated title and money, by being a technical expert. A scientist, for example, might be more motivated by having an opportunity to innovate and to work on outstanding teams with other world-class scientists rather than by being a manager or leader of other employees. As a leader, or future leader, it is critical to find out what motivates potential team members and appeal to that need, which will result in a far more effective team.

Most of us have been on teams that have a tight deadline. These days you just don't have the luxury of strategizing, assessing, and experimenting with what will work. And in many organizations you move from team to team with lightning speed—being assigned to the next project team before you have even completed the project you're working on. Especially for new team managers, this can be daunting. The best team leaders make sure that there's an environment of open communication—tension can be especially high when there's a deadline and a lot of pressure. They develop a system that works for the team. It may be structured time every week to share progress reports and assessments or more often an impromptu situation. They encourage open sharing among team members. If there's an immediate problem for team members, there is a contact person, a buddy, or a sub-team that they can contact immediately so that their process isn't impeded. What about distractions? When teams are working long hours, there may be a break for a pizza, a quick videogame competition, or a game of pool. Getting together outside work develops camaraderie, and relationships can be essential when everyone is tired, cranky, and at the end of their rope.

Developing these relationships is critical when the stakes are high and everyone is at odds. One senior leader shares his experience of bringing together his team in a time of great crisis and a looming deadline:

A few years ago, I was in charge of the construction of a major, multi-million-dollar research center for my company in the United Kingdom. Because of heated arguments among the contractors, architects, and the company, the consensus of the team was, "It's going to be impossible to get this job done." But the opening ceremony had already been arranged, to be attended by Queen Elizabeth, a number of Nobel Laureates, and other dignitaries. Faced with a seemingly impossible goal, workdays of 15 to 18 hours, participants at each others' throats, personality issues, and a looming deadline, I was faced with a challenge.

However, I find that you can tell a lot about a person's leadership potential by putting them in a non-business-related environment. I'm a strong proponent of using friendly athletic activities and team-building exercises. Because of this impasse, I decided to design an outward-bound-type ropes course weekend to include the key players from the three respective parties—contractors, architect, and corporate team. I wanted to get them into another environment to build a cohesive team. The motto of the weekend was "Failure Is Not an Option." The message was "Do you want to be a part of this team, or do you want to leave?"

Many team leaders personally have experienced a situation wherein one of their less team-oriented or popular members turns out to be the most successful at his or her task. Ironically, the only team member to succeed in the ropes course objectives was far from being the most popular member of the team due to personality dynamics. (The moral of the story? Just because you don't particularly like someone doesn't mean that they don't have the best ideas or can't get the job done.)

When the team arrived back at work on Monday morning after their weekend together, I had a sign greeting them saying, "Put Your Heart into It." By the end of that week, construction plans were in place for the project. It was no longer three different entities— rather it was a team effort. Through introspection, the team members learned trust—and you could see the results-oriented commitment in their eyes. Although we had to fine-tune the organizational chart a bit, through intervention, caring, and giving resources and responsibilities, the job got done one week ahead of schedule.

A simple crystal plaque with the completion date etched into it was given to each of the team members. Years later, these grown men would still have tears of pride in their eyes if you discussed this accomplishment.

One participant shares her thoughts on motivating any team: "Successful leaders celebrate the successes of their teams and team members. In these highly uncertain times, employees can often feel fragile and insecure—it's important for them to feel success even in small doses." Another leader concurs, adding: "What has been especially helpful for me as a leader to motivate my team? An ability to understand and appreciate each person's potential to be a contributing member of a team and a willingness to do anything that I would ask other people to do. This type of what might be called 'servant leadership' has been a key to my ability to lead and build teams and organizations."

Another trend that many of our leaders talked about was the importance of action learning, giving emerging leaders and others real-world challenges to address—essentially throwing smart people into a situation to see what strategies they come up with. Somewhat different than case studies, which, although effective, still essentially address a past challenge, these action learning sessions are future-focused and often organization-specific, providing opportunities to actually come up with a viable, customized strategy for your own industry or organization. You have a lot of your own smart, talented minds working on your own challenges. One of our clients has an interesting leadership program that creates teams of outstanding emerging leaders, selected from among the top managers, to work on a particular project, one that is specifically not in their own division or area of expertise. Yet each person brings different skills and a different background. The program is not only an effective leadership development opportunity but also an opportunity to gather data and generate ideas for the viability of new products and services. Each team is assigned a coach, and at the end of the project, the team presents its findings and project proposals to senior management. This same process can be used successfully in a number of settings.

Likewise, several years ago, we were involved with a consulting class at Wharton in which student teams would work with actual clients on a range of projects—developing an integrated global marketing strategy for one firm, finding an outlet for a new kind of paint that resists water for another company, and so on. Twice a semester, the students would simulate a client presentation as a dry run to iron out the kinks and so forth, and the professor would invite a group of experts from a wide range of fields to offer their insights and suggestions or pose probing questions. Not only were the students fully prepared for their actual client presentation at the end of the semester, but they also had had the opportunity to explore every aspect of a new product launch or comprehensive global marketing strategy. In addition, these student groups from a number of majors and cultures were able to develop effective cross-functional global teams, a skill that would be well used in today's environment. The key in all these examples is putting smart people into an unfamiliar setting to see what they come up with.

GETTING THE BEST PEOPLE FOR THE TEAM: WHAT LEADERS ARE LOOKING FOR

A number of the leaders we interviewed said that it's a challenge to identify the potential leaders in an organization and then to motivate those potential leaders. In addition, you have to also enable the employees who probably never will be leaders to grow and develop to their fullest potential. It's usually fairly easy to identify the ones at the top, the 5 to 10 percent. But identifying the potential skills of the other 90 percent is tricky. Bosses, mentors, advocates, and sponsors must pay careful attention to employees to identify latent skills and competencies—as well as to encourage them to develop additional expertise. As one leader said: "I've always been involved in baseball, well for about 45 to 50 years. First in Little League, now in coaching, and the scenario never changes. On every team there are always one or two kids who are really great. Then there are probably five or so who are pretty good. There are another two or three who are okay and then another two or three who are not very good. And I see the same percentages all the time in business. The best team members always will do well, but every chief executive officer (CEO) has the issue of motivating—and getting the best from—all members of the team."

One executive says that delivering results is far and away the most important thing team members can do to get on the radar screen of leaders. In addition to pure intellectual horsepower, she's looking for people who can grasp a wide range of issues and topics and who can add dimensionality, a future scope. She also wants people to have the courage to take a stand—who can express an opinion, not only follow directions. She is looking for future leaders who can take initiative, who take risks, and who have an innate ability to learn and to discern issues and problems without waiting for direction. Another leader concurs:

I'm looking for people who can identify the issues when they're working with clients and then talk about the solutions. They need to be able to go from strategy—the 50,000-foot view—to the implementation. They need to think logically, set the hypothesis regarding the problem, get the data, and then make the most logical recommendations possible. However, in addition to their strong technical skills, they also need the soft skills for implementation, the people skills to influence others, to move mountains, to get people to do stuff. It's like a three-legged stool—I need people with the know-how, the rapport, and the influence to work with clients.

One issue that several leaders raised is the question of whether to bring in talent from the outside for key positions or keep current players on the team. Do you look for someone with a track record—a known commodity or someone with potential? It's often a question of culture or style. A number of leaders prefer to develop their own people further. However, what if the "usual suspects," the ones on every key team, don't reflect where the organization is going—or should be going? What if the culture is the problem? The team is essentially the people who make it up—their collective strengths and weaknesses. Their skills, knowledge, and behavior can either perpetuate an ineffective culture or generate a new and improved one. Many next-generation leaders who have begun to take on higher-level leadership roles are more open, question more, and don't just mirror past leaders. We have asked many of them why they believe that their approach is different from that of their predecessors. They have grown up—literally and figuratively—with a different set of standards, more diversity, and a different environment. For some of them it just makes sense to challenge the status quo. Knowing when to bring in "new blood," different ideas, and fresh perspectives into key teams is critical. This leadership decision can be what differentiates a good team from a great team. One senior leader adds his thoughts on developing a high-performance team:

> *I found that it was necessary to "fast-track" our presence in the United States, so I decided that it was better to bring in an outsider from my previous network, someone I knew well, who already had a proven track record in achieving what needed to be done in that market. He was a known commodity, so I felt that it minimized the downside risk of choosing the wrong person.*
>
> *In the product management and software development area, however, I decided that it was better to keep the current players and help them raise their game, because with the critical need to get product to market quicker and better, I felt more comfortable keeping and developing people who knew the company products and culture/style. Bringing in outsiders in these areas would have undoubtedly taken some time to get them up to speed on products and process, which could have risked momentum being lost in the development process—critical in a high-tech arena.*

One theme that we have heard increasingly is that of "making the tough choices" with regard to key people who are great performers with a bad attitude. In the (not-too-distant) past it was assumed that leadership style and personality didn't matter too much in top performers—as long as they delivered, their ego, arrogance, and temper would be tolerated. This is quickly beginning to change. When senior leaders are looking around their organizations for who they want on their teams, they're starting to make the tough decisions. As one leader adds: "You can only get so far these days with the prima donnas with the ego and attitude. Those bully tactics just don't work anymore—people are too smart; they won't put up with that anymore. It's okay when they're just an individual—you may be willing to say, 'I can handle him or I can deal with her because they're adding to our bottom line.' But then when you need someone to lead a team or project or department, they have just limited themselves—they can't go any higher. Even the clients don't want to work with them."

Another leader put it this way: "There are four categories of people you have to choose from for any team. First, the great performer with the great attitude. That's an easy one. Then you have the average performer with the great attitude. You need to work with them to see if you can bring up their performance from average to great. Third, you have the mediocre performer with the mediocre attitude. That's an easy one, too. Where you have the biggest challenge is with the great performer with the lousy attitude. You don't want to let them go, but increasingly we're making the tough choices on them, even if they're senior leaders. You need a fit with the culture." An executive in the financial industry adds:

When I took on my new position, I needed to build a cohesive team. In 18 months I had to fire several people who were dysfunctional leaders. In order to get a team to work together well, sometimes you have to make changes. Even Jack Welch fired some of his best friends.

As another leader underscores: "It's not a good idea to let everyone believe that you know everything, that you have all the answers. They may look to you for guidance or direction, but the truth is that your team members probably know a lot more about specific issues than you do. Everyone has a different role; they are all experts in their own area. My job is to bring everything together and put it into perspective and keep them focused—with a strategic goal in mind."

CREATING DIVERSE TEAMS: LEVERAGE YOUR RESOURCES

Employees in many organizations admit that they are bad at leveraging their diverse resources. Don't think just race or gender; we're talking about generation, culture, global, and people who think differently, with a different frame of reference or a new perspective. Leaders should embrace individual differences and focus on performance, learning, and development. There sometimes still can be a stereotype about diverse teams as if the goal involves a quota, something that "you have to do." However, the importance of diverse teams lies in what they offer—multiple perspectives on issues and problems. Leaders need to bring a team together that uses each member's unique perspective. A homogeneous team brings you to a quick solution, but a heterogeneous team gives you a richer result—it takes longer but delivers a better outcome.

No one will deny that it can be more difficult to lead a diverse team. One chief financial officer (CFO) says that she likes to use the Myers-Briggs Type Indicator to get a sense of the team. It identifies different personality and communication types, which is especially important when trying to develop a more diverse team culture. It's also helpful in determining who the more creative members are, or the more tactical members, or who can keep everyone motivated and upbeat, especially during a crisis or with a tight deadline looming. Other leaders use their networks to get some background information on people who haven't necessarily had the right opportunities to gain a lot of visibility yet. They start by asking around to see if certain names keep coming up when colleagues recommend people for a team.

It's easy when everyone has the same experiences, the same history, and the same perspectives—teams can come to consensus and move on. And that was fine 50 years ago. Today, however, it's about not always getting the same people on the same teams—leaders have to seek out new ideas and fresh perspectives. And this can be scary because those new perspectives potentially can lead anywhere. This means that leaders are on the line to decide whether to continue on the same path or change strategic direction completely based on what emerges from the team. However, the bottom line is still the same—organizations need to look at and reflect on the diversity of their market, their customers, their suppliers, and their partners to develop their competitive advantage.

In these varying contexts, leaders want to find the people with the right skills and the right fit. They must understand what's important for the team; they need to reflect the client or customer in meetings. As one young leader said:

> *Ninety percent of the time, when we have to get a team together, someone asks, "Okay, who shall we get for this team?" And the same names keep coming up. When I'm choosing people for my teams, I'm not necessarily looking for the ones everyone chooses for every team, the superstars. I look for the people who work their tails off, are smart, do a great job, and get results. When forming a team, I try to pull some of the junior folks out—I'm looking for good people who have the ability to learn, the ability to discern issues, find—and solve—problems, and work well with clients. I don't care if they're quiet. I want people who can look at something differently than we have in the past, think of approaches that haven't been done before, think outside the box. I want people who can influence others, motivate them into action.*

Another executive agrees: "Being an officer in the military taught me the value of teamwork and diversity. Everybody thinks of the Marines as being authoritarian, but they're not. It's team-oriented. In Viet Nam, I had 31 men in my first command, most of whom were disadvantaged minorities without a high school diploma. But you learned that disadvantaged didn't mean that they weren't smart. They *had* innate intelligence and character. You saw who the natural leaders were. You just had to recognize their skill sets and bring out those individual strengths of your team members."

READY. . . FIRE . . . AIM

One problem that we have heard with a lot of teams is that many people jump into an assignment, project, or task without thinking first about the goal, the process, and the right people needed for the best result. They just want to get started—they want to *do* something. You just have to watch a couple of episodes of *The Apprentice* to prove this point—many project teams seem to start rushing around, coming up with instant solutions without taking the time to think and plan—and most of the time they're running around like chickens without heads. But there is a process. Especially when you have a lot of very smart people together, they often don't want to go through the process—they want action. Ready, fire, aim. Lack of planning, especially at the beginning of any team, can lead to a lot of confusion, people going off in the wrong direction, and misunderstanding of what the leader wants—the team is missing the mark. Leaders have to make sure that everyone knows exactly what the task and goal are and what they need to deliver in terms of results.

Author Gary Klein shares a situation in which military team leaders at the Army War College and the National Defense University were given a task to complete—one that would be timed and competitive:[2]

Most of the team leaders, anxious to get a head start on the competition, rushed through their instructions and got everyone working. As one might imagine, there were a lot of questions and subteams going off in the wrong direction, misunderstanding what the team leader wanted, causing time delays and frustration. However, one leader spent 15 minutes making sure that everyone knew exactly what the task was and what he wanted. Despite the time constraints, he didn't rush. His team didn't go off in the wrong direction and didn't make costly errors. They were effective because they received clear direction from the beginning. Interestingly, one of the other teams started the first day's activities with only 90 seconds of direction. Of course, there were lots of mistakes that day. The next day the team leader took 10 minutes for direction. And on the third he spent 15 minutes. He learned from his mistakes, realizing that spending the time planning and giving direction pays off down the road.

Another leader added: "I spend 50 percent of my allotted time planning, 25 percent doing, and 25 percent evaluating."

However, one executive gives this advice to team leaders:

It's best not to give lots of unnecessary details—they can further confuse what you want to accomplish. Leaders want to encourage independent thinking within given guidelines and let other people come up with interesting ways of getting the job done. You just want the results. Provide some reasoning as to why you want your team to do something, but keep it concise. Don't give them a laundry list of reasons. It is important not to mistake encouragement or cheerleading with intent. Rather than simply saying something like, "Our goal is to be Number One!" provide a strategy and specific goals.

CHAPTER SUMMARY

Success Secret #9: Building and Leading High-Performance Teams

♦ In addition to skills, knowledge, and experience, team leaders should consider the intangibles when choosing a team: passion, thinking about issues from a different perspective, having the courage to take a stand and challenge others, and the ability to think logically, to inspire, and to persuade.

♦ Team leaders have to consider the right mix of people: personalities, culture, and perspectives. They must consider not only the individuals but also the chemistry of the team—the "collective genius."

♦ Increasingly, organizations need to bring people together in teams from different functions, even different industries, to apply new thinking to a problem or challenge.

♦ Team members are motivated by things other than money and perks. They often find reward in contributing to a collaborative effort—being part of a world-class team that makes a real difference.

- Give a smart team a future-focused, organizationally centered challenge and see what solutions they come up with. Use your "collective genius" for competitive advantage.

- Organizations are becoming less tolerant of ego and bad attitude—even with their best performers. People are too smart and won't put up with such behavior anymore. Clients don't want to work with such people, and team leaders don't want to deal with them.

- Planning is essential for effective teams. The best leaders take time to set goals and plan strategy for execution—more time planning, less time doing—and undoing.

Leading—and Thriving—in an Environment of Ambiguity, Uncertainty, and Change

In one press conference, Donald Rumsfeld, Secretary of Defense, spoke about something with which we are dealing in every corner of the world—that is leading in an environment of ambiguity, uncertainty, and change. He said

It's one thing to say there are known knowns, here are the things we know we know and let's talk about them and let's arrange them into estimates and make sure the people have that information. There's another category of known unknowns. We know we don't know certain things. And that's good to know. It's almost as good as knowing what you know, to know what you don't know. . . . But there's a whole other category and that's the unknown unknowns. They're the things you don't know you don't know. And that is the problem. And what you need is to have people thinking about those things in a way that's fresh and different.

Actually, the speech was delivered as somewhat of a tongue-in-cheek commentary, but the content is nonetheless accurate. Essentially, what leaders need in this environment is a bunch of people who aren't confined by the usual constraints of logical thinking. You need blue sky, outside-the-box thinkers considering things that the rest of us have never even imagined, let alone come up with solutions for. These are the innovators who don't know that they're not supposed to do something—that something can't be done. You don't necessarily want them leading the team, but it's good to have them on the team.

Using Secretary Rumsfeld's analogy that introduced this chapter, organizations traditionally have understood their environments—their "known knowns and unknowns." Although the situation frequently was uncertain, there was usually at least an expectation of what the uncertainties were—the players changed, the "cause" changed, but the drivers, motivators, and strategies were often pretty much the same. Leaders could be called on from either a military background or a civilian background but largely were chosen based on what they had done in the past—their experiences, their positions, their successes, and how they had handled previous situations. They were not usually chosen based on the potential for what they *could* do or *might be able* to do in a given situation. (However, even in the past there was the occasional leader who didn't necessarily have what people would consider traditional skills from traditional backgrounds—the unexpected leader. Some may not even have had traditional preparation for a leadership role. In the American Civil War, for example, some of the most successful leaders included college professors, corporate executives, underachievers, and has-beens.)

Fast forward to the twenty-first century. Unlike in the past when most leaders were evaluated based on their past performance, in today's times of crisis, leaders are needed who can succeed in situations in which uncertainty and even chaos are acute. Some of the most dramatic aspects of leading today will be in the midst of unprecedented changes in technology, globalization, and heightened competition worldwide—it's difficult to even project at this time just how rapidly an environment can change. In the same way that cutting-edge technology becomes obsolete in 18 months or less, so too can we anticipate that the rate of change will increase. This time of uncertainty and rapid change requires flexibility, responsiveness, and innovation, necessitating leaders who may be from different backgrounds, with diverse perspectives, skills, competencies, knowledge, or a style that may be somewhat unorthodox.

Interestingly enough, although some people have remarked that we should look for an alternative to the prevailing (and presumably) military model, which assumes a rigid, hierarchical environment where people don't think outside the box, we have often found quite the opposite in interviewing many leaders who do come from military backgrounds. As one of our participants added: "A lot of officers in the Marines are 'F's' and 'P's' [in Myers-Briggs Type Indicator terms]—there's a lot of big-picture thinking going on."

While we're on the topic of the military—they have an acronym for operating in the increasingly complex, uncertain environment of the future—VUCA. Volatility. Uncertainty. Complexity. Ambiguity. Change today is not only ongoing but also accelerating. We just have to get used to it. We can't accurately predict what is going to happen. We need to become even more aware of how issues and events are interconnected. It's increasingly difficult to know where to focus our strategies—a "ready, fire, aim" approach seems to have become the strategy of choice for many. However, the environment is not going to change, so leaders have to address this relatively new phenomenon by developing—and practicing— the right skills.

THE RIGHT SKILLS

Most leaders have acknowledged that they are facing a highly complex set of challenges. Management was created for organizational stability, efficiency, and performance that is at least somewhat predictable—and ironically, this is how most organizations still run their business. However, some leaders understand—some don't—that a new set of skills, competencies, knowledge, and behaviors is required to respond to the new challenges. This is unknown territory for most—they now lead strategic change without clear guidelines in an uncertain and rapidly changing world. They can no longer rely on a comfort level of predictable structures and controls. Increasingly, success depends on the ability to manage change—"You have to learn, grow, and change faster than the competition." It's about risk and reward. Those who have the risk tolerance—and can deliver results—will stand to gain considerable competitive advantage.[1] As one participant adds: "Leaders today face more complex challenges: a 24/7 world, globalization, instantaneous need for instant information, efficiency, productivity, doing more with less. There are shorter cycles; time is a precious commodity. They have to be masters at strategy and tactical at the same time." Another leader gives his thoughts on this environment:

Today's leaders must be accepting of change—and the accelerating pace of change. Individuals' leadership capabilities are impeded if they are not accepting of challenges and risks. If you're not at least a little scared, you're not optimizing opportunities for yourself and the firm.

Leaders have to create a strategy to motivate and share their values and vision. In addition, many of our participants added that they are looking for leaders who have the courage to challenge the status quo—they want people who can ask the tough questions and cause others to think differently, outside the box. Continuous learning also was high on our leaders' agendas—the world is changing so quickly that it's harder to anticipate potential opportunities and threats. Leaders must be able to switch gears quickly—and accurately—so organizations worldwide need leaders who can think, analyze, anticipate, and react without losing focus or heading in the wrong direction (or at least be able to recover quickly if they do). In the early days of the Internet, Bill Gates wasn't convinced that this was the way for Microsoft to go. However, when he realized its impact, his courage and flexibility allowed him to shift gears quickly and go all-out, largely capturing the market.

A top executive at General Motors shared the same approach as the company faced a radical change in the automotive paradigm:

One challenge we had as an organization was looking beyond the technology that we have been using for more than 100 years, the internal combustion engine. Developing fuel cell technology, with its more efficient, zero emissions advantages, necessitated a fundamental change in the way we built cars.

We had to tell our people that in 20 to 30 years, the whole environment would change. It's when, not if. We had to figure out how to start causing that to happen. We set up two research centers and brought in scientists and engineers from diverse fields: automotive, chemical, aerospace, and others—innovative people who were not committed to the way we built cars. There was no baggage from the past. They didn't necessarily have to know anything about gasoline engines, but they knew fuel cells.

We had to create a new work environment focusing on intellectual freedom. We gave our people the necessary resources and created a more high-tech model. The next step was to bring together the technology people and the automotive engineers to work collaboratively on how to manufacture in volume. The cultural change was an important ingredient. There was a transition period, but the "old timers" had become believers. They needed to see results—and they did.

Unlike in the past, leaders now have to sort through overwhelming amounts of information, focus on the most important issues, make decisions from a number of possible options, and choose the right course of action. Prioritizing challenges and choosing the right ones to focus on will be essential—and increasingly difficult in an uncertain, sometimes volatile environment. Without the luxury of predictability, leaders today also need to be nimble—ready to respond to challenges and identify strategic issues in ambiguous situations. And we're not talking just in the lightning world of technology. Even in more mature, stable organizations, situations can change overnight. Suppliers suddenly can become competitors, industry innovations instantly can make your product obsolete, and the omnipresent shroud of terrorism threatens seemingly unlikely targets. The more precarious the situation, the greater is the need for leaders to quickly assess the situation and make informed decisions, often with little data available. Every leader will have to respond quickly to unexpected change. For example, the recent Atkins' diet craze, at the height of its popularity, significantly affected decision making among leaders at a number of food and beverage manufacturers, who had to ask themselves if this was just a fad or the next phase of the industry. Some jumped on the bandwagon, often without a well-thought-out business model for sustained growth, whereas others decided to take a wait-and-see attitude. Several years later it seems to have become yet the latest diet craze in which only the strongest new product lines will survive. Some leaders gambled and lost.

But as several of our participants added, many chief executive officers (CEOs) and other key executives often operate in survival mode at best, thinking—and acting—reactively rather than proactively. Yet, in a world of mergers and acquisitions, dramatic marketplace shifts, and major strategic and organizational change, it has become increasingly difficult to sidestep the issue. There are fewer and fewer "textbook" leadership behaviors that you can use—case-study approaches can prepare leaders for the types of situations that have already happened, the type of challenges we already know about, but you're basically "fighting the last war." Leaders must prepare for challenges we can't even conceive of—and that's the hard part. Increasingly, leaders at every level have to hone their flexibility, their communication skills, and their ability to see the big picture and connect seemingly unrelated situations to prepare them for the unexpected. As one of our participants commented: "You choose what you think are the best strategies, make decisions based on them, and stay flexible. You can't eliminate the uncertainty; you just have to deal with it and make the best decisions you can." Some leaders may be able to go with their gut feeling or experience; others use formal assessments to test their comfort level with uncertainty. Although some leaders feel that they have too little information to make decisions confidently, many leaders complain that they are on information overload.

More than ever, approaches to leadership will be contextual. People have to ask themselves, "What is the right leadership approach for this particular context?" It's increasingly important to look at skill sets, knowledge, and behaviors of the leader needed for a given situation rather than considering a specific individual on the basis of his position or past accomplishments. One of our leaders adds that she always looks for the skill set first when choosing key team members. She confirms that it is critical to consider who the best members should be based on what they bring to the table, not necessarily what they have done in the past. Do they have the right style for the project? Are they focused on the process or the results? Do they have the ability to see the big picture, to ask tough questions, analyze, connect concepts, and come up with logical solutions in seeming chaos? Do they have the courage to challenge established leaders or conventions or show confidence that they believe their course of action is the right one to take? Can they persuade others to take that action? Do they have the risk tolerance to stay the course? Can they keep others calm and confident in their decisions? Now more than ever leaders frequently need to depend on intangible traits—courage, confidence, persuasion, logic, and instinct—rather than merely their experience to gain that competitive edge.

BEYOND UNCERTAINTY: CRISIS

Since it's clear that we no longer live in a predictable world, we can't prepare leaders solely by sharing what has worked well in the past. But if you asked leaders, "Do you think that your environment will become more certain or ambiguous in the next 5 to 10 years, more turbulent or more calm?" you can bet what their responses will be. Given that likelihood, developing strategies on how to best deal with ambiguity, uncertainty, turbulence, and chaos is even more critical. Leaders have to leverage uncertainty. They need to ascertain what specific behaviors can help them to operate more effectively when they find themselves in this environment—improving communication, exhibiting calm under fire, a positive, confident style, showing empathy, and making sense of chaos. They must be adaptable and nimble. We can prepare our future leaders for the *process* of dealing with uncertainty by giving them the right tools and the right guidance to deal with future challenges. Senior leaders have to build the environment that enables this type of critical thinking and thoughtful—but often rapid—decision making to take place, allowing their teams to navigate the uncertainties that lie ahead. It should become part of the culture. It's important to make sure that everyone is on the same wavelength and can react quickly in a crisis.

The more uncertain the environment and the more ambiguous the issue requiring a decision, the more leadership is needed—not just technical skills, but communication, relationship-building, seeing the "big picture," analysis, diagnosis, and execution. One situation that typifies this type of environment occurred at Bearing Point. On September 11, 2001, where there were over 250 Bearing Point people in the World Trade Center and in surrounding buildings and 15 people at the Pentagon. CEO Rand Blazer praised his team:

What was great about our team was that there were leaders in New York and D.C. who quickly assessed that something was wrong and quickly organized a central center for action and information. Within minutes, they took quick action and told everyone to evacuate. Not only at the World Trade Center and the Pentagon but also at the State Department, White House, etc. Managing Partners Sarah Diamond, Dan Johnson, and Rich Roberts took the leadership roles and organized the operation, establishing a sort of command center.

As soon as the event occurred, individual leaders became apparent throughout the organization. They assessed, acted, and reacted quickly, saying, "I think we have situation here; let's move, let's get out, start making your way home. . . ." Many of the employees were on the sixty-something floor. Our employees were told to ignore the statements that it was okay to return to work—they were told, "Just get down to the ground floor." Our many leaders that day looked at the situation quickly and systematically using a model: diagnostic, interpretation, decision making, execution. Every employee in the World Trade Center was safely evacuated. In addition, a call was made to every major office in the United States—often getting people out of bed—telling them what to do. In San Francisco, for example, we told our people, "Stay at home today—work from home, stay out of the downtown. . . ."

These leaders were able to diagnose the situation on the spot, and move, react. They realized that the difference in action can save people's lives—and certainly in this case it did. Our corporate culture is that we have to have leaders across the environment; leadership is decentralized—it's not by accident that they took the leadership roles in a crisis and did it well. And it was not necessarily senior management. Segment or industry leaders took charge of situations, made quick decisions, and acted. Employees at the consultant level wouldn't leave until everyone was accounted for. . . .

We asked Mr. Blazer if he felt that his personal—and positive—experience as a military officer had helped him become a role model, making an impact on the corporate culture, filtering down and encouraging this type of leadership. He said, "I don't want to take credit for these leaders' actions. It wasn't a corporate decision. These individuals did an amazing job—they assessed the situation and acted immediately." A true leader, giving credit to his team and not taking credit himself, his experience undoubtedly has greatly influenced the culture overall—one of the underlying themes at the organization is to constantly encourage leadership at all levels. "It is not bureaucratic; they don't have to go up and down the ladder; there is a clear delegation of leadership."

PREPARING FOR AMBIGUITY, VOLATILITY, AND CHANGE

Researchers have come up with three categories of dealing with uncertainty, the first being *macro uncertainties,* things over which we have little or no control (such as war, unanticipated global issues, recession, and so on).[2] However, although we can't precisely anticipate the timing, we can be pretty darn sure that there could be another terror attack, recession, or war. Organizations must prepare for these possibilities. Some companies caught in the World Trade Center disaster had their backup systems right next door. Not much good. However, financial firms and many others now have instituted extensive disaster recovery plans that anticipate this possibility—selecting extensively redundant backup systems and alternate sites in other states (even thinking about such issues as, "We don't have to cross a body of water to get to the backup site—just in case the bridges are out of commission." (But even this is reactive—what organizations really should be thinking about and planning for is what *hasn't* happened yet, what they haven't anticipated—that's the hard part. As Donald Rumsfeld says, these are the "unknown unknowns.")

Industry uncertainties make up the second category—the events over which organizations have some control (such as competitors, consumers, suppliers, and partners). Leaders can't necessarily predict what others will do. However, some of the uncertainty can be reduced with effective communication, understanding consumer needs, developing relationships to better work with suppliers, understanding emerging market demands, and so forth. Some uncertainty can be reduced with research—do we really know everything we need to know about the market, present and future? Do we have analytical people who can anticipate future trends or market moves? Do we know our competitive market advantage—or are we working on expanding it? Developing wider networks can provide greater insights—new people with a fresh perspective of how things could be done, who is in your market, and how to capture additional market share. Better understanding of emerging trends or issues can reduce uncertainty. Likewise, organizations have to find the pulse point of what customers are thinking—how they will respond to your actions. Those who are closer to customers are most likely to get a better sense of what their audience needs and wants—listen to them.

The third category, *internal uncertainties,* are within our organizations (our resources, deadlines, or budgets, for example). This should be the easiest category to demystify. Communication, developing relationships, and building trust all contribute significantly to minimizing the unknowns. (Is it real uncertainty, or is it just something I don't know at this time? Leaders need to be able to differentiate between the two.) They should get out and talk to people, do a little homework, and create opportunities to learn.

We know that some readers are thinking that this is stating the obvious— that every leader knows what he needs to be doing. The thing is—they may know, but many organizations still aren't doing it. Leaders know that they ought to, but are they really taking everything into consideration to prepare for uncertainty on a sociocultural, political, legal, and economic basis? What were the contingency plans in place at major banks to deal with the economic issues over the past few years in Russia, Argentina, and Japan? What about oil companies operating in Saudi Arabia, Iraq, and elsewhere in the Middle East? These and many other organizations obviously are thinking about their doomsday scenarios, but more important, they have to consider *who* is in on the development of them. Are these organizations getting insights from people who see the issue from various perspectives, who are thinking outside the box, the people whose approaches may seem unorthodox? Often based on tacit knowledge (the "underground network" of who you want on your team—who really can get the job done), this decision of whom to choose for key teams comes partly from knowing which leaders have the right skills and knowledge. It's not a case study— senior leaders need to assess each situation and focus on who can do it, not just go with "usual suspects" for every key team. Leaders can't plan for the future by fighting the last war. However, as one of our participants added:

New leaders also have to be aware that ideas that are too radical will never gain buy-in from the team. Leaders finding themselves in this situation should introduce breakthrough strategies within the established parameters of decision making, at least in the beginning.

It's also critically important to get the right team together that has not only the appropriate complementary skills for that situation but also the right chemistry, the intangibles. Organizations need leadership that can see the big picture, make sure that the right people are involved, put the right systems in place, and be able to execute. More than this, though, it's essential to know which leaders are known for their risk tolerance, their ability to learn, their confidence, their ability to lead, inspire, and remain calm in a crisis, and their ability to communicate that everything will be okay in the end. Probably

Winston Churchill's greatest talent was his ability to communicate ultimate victory to the people of Great Britain—that despite whatever hardship, they ultimately would be victorious. Rudy Guiliani did not have the specific *experience* needed to deal with the September 11 tragedy, but he did have the right skills—and the right behaviors and style. He showed empathy, he communicated frequently and from the heart, and he instilled confidence.

A number of the leaders we interviewed talked about how they choose certain people for various strategic positions. In addition to the normal facts that you want to get out of the interview, they do more probing, asking more descriptive questions. Have you ever led a turnaround assignment? How have you dealt with—and recovered from—a failure? Give some details about your experience. There are certain people—probably not that many—who are comfortable in and indeed seek out projects that have an element of risk or uncertainty. It's the thrill and challenge of the unknown. And this is why they're such a hot commodity.

One of our leaders shared his advice about taking risks and making decisions:

> *Less experienced leaders have to take risks to learn—you can't let risks slow you down. If you make a wrong decision and then spend too much time worrying about the consequences, it adversely affects how you approach making your next decision. Don't be paralyzed. Make your decision and move on.*

In environments of uncertainty, are people in your organization allowed to fail? As one of our participants said: "Managers often tell their people, 'Don't worry—we've never killed anyone here for making a mistake!' But that's not true—they can and do kill your advancement." What really happens in your environment if you fail—what are the ramifications? Does it depend on the scope and magnitude of the failure—is it really a career-breaker? Does it depend on who is doing the failing—do certain people have influential sponsors who put a safety net around their decisions? What's the real message—the ingrained culture? One of our leaders gives this advice:

> *Take risks and have failures earlier in your career when the stakes are lower. Practice risk taking when it doesn't count as much. The more success you have, the more failures they can tolerate with you— it's dollar cost averaging. And you gain a lot of confidence with each success that builds on itself.*

Some leaders believe that success depends largely on the culture, the environment. In some organizations, a degree of failure is acceptable—it's a natural part of learning the risk-taking process—in others, it's a black mark on your record. Maybe you can fail once, even twice, but a pattern isn't seen as a good thing. Our participants recommend that if you're going to take a chance, get buy-in from senior people. They need to feel comfortable taking a chance with you. They advise younger leaders to score early wins—a good track record may give them the necessary halo effect to take chances and fail. The organization is willing to give you another chance.

UNCERTAINTY, AMBIGUITY, CHANGE, AND EMOTIONAL INTELLIGENCE

A number of our participants talked about their leadership roles in uncertain or turbulent times. Although such an environment can be, for some, a time of excitement and challenge, more frequently it includes stress, fear, lack of control, and anxiety for even the most seasoned leader. In this highly stressful, emotional setting, many followers—and some leaders—react with insecurity and even anger. Several leaders told us: "It's easy to lead when times are okay. But true leadership comes out in tough times." Some people draw inward—instead of communicating, they hide in their proverbial office, become negative, and blame others for the situation. Conversely, our leaders communicate even more frequently with all their stakeholders in times of uncertainty and stress—employees, customers, shareholders, and the public. A number of our leaders also underscored the importance of being authentic leaders, especially in times of uncertainty—getting people together, talking from the heart, and letting people know you care. How the message is delivered is extremely important—is it harsh, with little emotion and a lack of empathy, or is it authentic and compassionate? This is what gets people through tough times. One participant recounted his advice to an emerging leader overseeing his first unavoidable staff reduction:

I try to help leaders come to their own decisions by asking the question, "Is the decision the right thing for both the employees and the business? If so, then there's no choice." Although he was very upset at having to make cuts, he handled it with great empathy and ultimately realized that he had made the best decision.

Authentic leaders like these appeal to people's "higher selves." They instill positive emotions around performance. They're aware of what's going on, understand the emotions of their people, and earn their trust. They move toward solutions and help others to move as well. They "up the communication level." They have self-awareness, and they listen as well as speak. Despite their own apprehensions, they are outwardly calm, positive, "talking to the troops, telling them that they are going to get through this." They are aware of the emotions, rumors, and fears, recognizing the challenges, difficulties, and turbulence but building a sense of optimism that "everything will be okay." As one participant states:

> *Leaders must show that they have a genuine interest in the health, welfare, and well-being of their people. In the case of major changes in the organization, particularly when they involve layoffs, it's best to be upfront and honest—employees can take the bad news. If discussions only take place behind closed doors, people know that something's up. There's a vacuum of information—if you don't fill it with facts, it fills with rumor.*

Interestingly, our leaders also underscored the significance of their own physical and mental state, citing the importance of being, as one participant called it, "energy givers, not energy drainers." They create a positive environment, focusing on positive goals and "caring for their people." It helps their team to deal with the uncertainty. Good leaders know how to manage these emotions and move on. Although, as Donald Rumsfeld says, the future is unknowable, leaders can learn how to cope with change through resilience and communication.

The bottom line: It's hard to predict what uncertainties lie ahead. What leaders need to do is to create an environment in which preparation, quick thinking, the ability to analyze the situation, and excellent communication skills are already in place.

CHAPTER SUMMARY

Success Secret #10: Leading—and Thriving—in an Environment of Ambiguity, Uncertainty, and Change

♦ Leaders must be able to anticipate emerging trends by seeing the "big picture," connecting the dots on numerous pieces of information. Leader strategy must reflect and constantly accommodate a changing marketplace and increasing external threats and opportunities.

♦ Leaders need to share their vision and enable an open, learning culture in order to create competitive advantage and thrive in a complex, rapidly changing environment.

♦ Organizations should identify leaders who have a new and different perspective when faced with uncertainty and change. They must leverage these new and innovative ideas. In addition, they should consider a range of leadership behaviors and characteristics in addition to skills, experience, and knowledge.

♦ It is essential to develop, enable, and encourage a learning environment focused on different ways of doing things, building relationships, and mentoring.

♦ Leaders should be prepared to look at the "big picture" and make decisions with limited information.

♦ In order to manage uncertainty more effectively, leadership elements, such as leader presence and communication, have to increase.

Final Thoughts

When we started this book, we had some general ideas about what we thought we would find in terms of leadership from talking to colleagues and clients, the literature, previous trends in our research, and so forth. However, what surprised us was the extent to which the very model of leadership seemingly has changed just in the past 10 years or so. While it probably will take another decade to filter down in some organizations—and indeed start to click with the senior leadership of others—the fact remains that leaders ought to be looking closely at the dramatic changes that are happening right now.

What are some of the major issues? First is the critical—and we mean *critical*—shortage of future talent with the appropriate combination of technical skills and those intangible skills. The research definitely mirrors reality—leaders we spoke to are desperate for a certain type of next generation leader. We really began to think more critically about this, looking carefully at the people who would be considered the "gold collar" workers so much in demand now versus the typical smart, technically sound people that are in—and lead—many organizations today. Many of those who were considered the gold standard 10 or 20 years ago—the bottom-line, just get it done, kick butt, and take names later leaders—just can't cut it now. Why not? Organizations today are desperate for leaders who can deal with uncertainty, have a global perspective, and work well in a diverse environment, diverse frames of reference and perspectives, and stakeholder diversity in race, culture, gender, and more. Today it's about future focus, seeing the "big picture," and planning strategically with a lot of moving parts.

Many leaders talk about their pool of "smart people"—yes, there are a lot of smart people out there. We talk to smart people all the time, but in some there's something missing—they just don't get it. What many people haven't quite grasped yet, we believe, is that while being smart and technically competent is essential for leaders, it's a given—technical skills become a smaller percentage of what leaders need to lead in the future. What are clearly missing among many leaders are the intangible leadership skills—passion, persuasion, energy, emotional intelligence, resilience, the ability to deal with complexity and make decisions in ambiguous environments, the courage to question the status quo, and the compassion to care about their people. There becomes an inverse relationship between the respective importance of technical skills/basic intellect and the intangible aspects of leadership as individuals move into higher leadership positions.

We loved the idea of the Aspen Institute and the Educational Leadership Program focusing on liberal arts—leaders coming together to actually practice critical thinking and read Plato. We feel the same about smart, passionate young people getting a lot of their friends and colleagues together and starting their own think tanks. It was very telling when an extraordinarily insightful and successful business leader said that she needed to be broader based in terms of reading more—and on more diverse topics such as history— to better connect with her executive-level clients. A number of our chief executive officers (CEOs) talked about the importance of being broad-based not just in business but also in such things as philosophy and theology (to better understand ethics and the importance of developing a moral compass) and history (to get a frame of reference on great leadership—concepts that are still valid today). Studying foreign languages, foreign culture, and classic literature gives a more comprehensive view of other perspectives and diverse ways of thinking.

It will take inspired leadership to move these ideas forward, to change the culture to one that values learning and enables individuals to challenge themselves—and others—in a positive environment that fosters shared information and diverse cross-functional teams. There are many people in organizations that have these broad skills—and many of them have not yet been identified. It is critical for leaders to dig a little deeper to see who is out there and what talent lies just beneath the surface waiting to be developed and nurtured. The environment is changing around us—leaders no longer have the luxury to take their time—they need to address these issues right away.

Best Practices in Creating Successful Leaders

One issue was virtually unanimous among our participants—successful leadership is not an individual undertaking. All leaders depend on the accomplishments of their teams for their own individual success. And increasingly, the responsibility for creating successful leaders is being taken on by leaders themselves—leadership learning is no longer seen as the sole domain of the training and human resources departments.

A number of people we spoke to wanted to know what other organizations are doing to prepare their leaders. So we have invited our participants to share some of their best practices for preparing successful leaders. Whether they have chosen to be recognized for their initiatives or have elected to remain anonymous, these insights reflect how many of the top organizations in their fields are maximizing their leadership talent.

For established leaders, you will read about new strategies that you can put into practice to improve your own team's performance and satisfaction.

And for you emerging leaders—many executives and career advisors emphasize that you should be proactive about creating your own career path. This section will give you insights into the types of leadership initiatives that many organizations make available. Use this information to investigate leadership opportunities—either formal or informal—in your own workplace. Take the initiative to ask your boss about introducing new leadership programs in your department or in your team. And remember, as you take on greater leadership responsibilities of your own, one of your most important roles is to support the generation of leaders coming up behind you.

For our readers who are leadership development practitioners, you undoubtedly will benefit from benchmarking—and hopefully validating—your own initiatives.

In the following excerpts from our participant interviews, thought leaders from top organizations worldwide describe how they address their leadership needs.

IBM

Building a model of leadership development critically involves defining the competencies that differentiate outstanding versus average performance. Our world is shifting again—now it's about "on demand" development of new competencies for a specific organization. IBM has 30,000 leaders focused on competencies, the development process, and learning solutions. As a common thread at the heart of this are our values: innovation, client focus, trust, and personal responsibility. Three examples of our 10 leadership competencies define behavior and are very demanding: thinking horizontally, collaborative influence, and taking strategic risks.

Work-based learning is a way to get scale. Our leaders mentor and teach. Development covers 40 topics over a two-year period, preparing people to take on leadership opportunities and to gain role models. With each transition come more opportunities for emerging leaders to benefit from more world-class, advanced leadership topics presented in a blended approach to learning. Up the line to leader of leaders, the focus is on how leaders develop and assess other leaders. It's a strategy for the executive-level position that has responsibility over multiple layers. For the preexecutive, business simulations are used. Each part of the leadership development continuum has a tested, facilitated dialogue that includes a preclass and postclass learning assessment.

We have just launched an approach, which we call *PARR,* that involves four steps for learning at IBM: *Prepare, Act, Reflect, and Review.* It is focused not just on moving quickly but on considering lessons learned, keeping an online journal, and other reflective pieces. It accelerates the process, sparks new ideas and innovation—a so-called learning "blog" that can be public or private. Core programs for emerging leaders concentrate on personalized learning that helps to strengthen individual competencies. You can go to a particular Web site or take a prescriptive class through multiple channels to have a work-based or online experience. PARR is the core of an entirely integrated approach. It is available to everyone, which is critical to ensure pervasive innovation on a daily basis. In an increasingly fast-paced world, we want people to think, to reflect, and to convey their thinking in the review process. Learning is beyond courses—it involves pervasive practices.

UBS

In 2001, UBS saw the launch of the UBS Leadership Institute as a key part of company strategy. It was granted the mandate to expand and enhance the firm's leadership development capabilities and alignment, specifically for the top-level management talent.

The UBS Leadership Institute focuses on the UBS Group Executive and Group Management Boards, plus the top 600 senior managers and selected high potentials of the firm. Through our programs and initiatives, we promote positive culture change and equip UBS's senior leadership to achieve the firm's vision to be recognized as the best global financial services company. Our programs and initiatives are directly aligned to UBS's strategy and globally focused, emphasizing developing leaders across the firm's various business groups.

Two high-level forums aimed at the UBS Group Executive and Managing Boards and top managers are the yearly annual strategic forum and the senior leadership conference. The objective is to create firm-wide understanding and alignment around our vision and values, integrated business model, and strategic direction.

Our suite of global leadership experience (GLE) programs were designed for the top 600 senior managers and are focused, respectively, on understanding the total enterprise (GLE I), building and leveraging organizational capabilities (GLE II), and building leadership capabilities (GLE III). Feedback, coaching, and learning are integral parts of each program, with leaders throughout the firm serving as coaches, teachers, and participants.

The accelerated leadership experience (ALE) is our newest offering for selected members of the firm's high-potentials pipeline. The program is built around developing UBS's three core competencies of client focus, entrepreneurial leadership, and partnering for organic growth in the next generation of leaders. This program includes extensive prework, as well as completion of a 360-degree feedback instrument and professional coaching/mentoring for participants both during and after the program.

Our leadership development forums and programs are augmented through senior-level mentoring programs and our advisory work in areas such as innovation and knowledge and developing value propositions. The real thread of commonality throughout our work is support of the "One Firm" ideal through facilitating the sharing of ideas, knowledge, experience, and expertise across business groups, functions, and regions. We believe that our efforts have produced some measurable, concrete results in aligning top management behind a common UBS vision and strategic business direction. We also have seen increasing internal and external recognition of our work that includes receiving the Corporate University Xchange's award for "Best Launch of a New Corporate University."

ACCENTURE

We have a formal leadership statement that articulates what an Accenture leader is—a very thoroughly written document that is supported by our performance management and rewards system. There is a very tight linkage between the organization's leadership strategy and all our leadership development initiatives.

We strive to have the appropriate development program for every level of leader and use active learning as a key feature of our training programs. Programs are also highly targeted—for diverse employee populations, different geographic regions, and so forth. Programs are made more effective by providing clear expectations, measuring people against them, and rewarding people for successfully achieving their goals.

We put a strong focus on the individual. We've seen that successful leaders enjoy the opportunity to learn about themselves. They understand emotional intelligence issues and want to know how they are perceived and what causes someone to behave in a certain way. They want to make meaningful relationships. We therefore focus heavily on building confidence and communication skills.

We measure the success of our leaders based on our leadership statement, balancing assessments around three characteristics: the individual's ability to create value, to develop people, and to operate the business effectively. We also measure the effectiveness of our leadership development training by asking participants if the development initiatives have made a difference to them and how they approach leadership in their job as a result. We take a diagnostic approach, asking if there are other things that we need to provide or what they could do to develop themselves further.

MERRILL LYNCH

Our CEO has demonstrated a strong bottom-line commitment to developing our company's leaders. Under his sponsorship, we are bringing about cultural change that involves creating a new language around leadership. Our leadership development plan is grounded in the strategies of the firm and very future-focused—we are working in a three- to five-year horizon. We are examining ways of closing gaps by determining what talent we need.

To support our leaders, we take an action learning approach of combining classroom and fieldwork experiences that reflect the real world. For example, we develop customized case studies that can be implemented in our firm. Our programs are designed to take advantage of the best internal and external resources. We have a formal program to enable our experienced leaders to take on roles as faculty members. They act as internal facilitators, executive coaches, and sponsors. These leaders are highly engaged and carve out a significant amount of time to take part in the development process. This approach is viewed by our employees as collaborative, reaching across the organization, rather than simply as a human resources program.

Our leadership development initiatives are based on four competencies that we consider necessary to form a well-rounded leader: focusing on excellence, understanding and driving strategy, delivering business results, and demonstrating strong people leadership.

We believe that if you can't measure it, you can't improve. Our leadership development programs are highly outcomes-based—performance measurements are built into our program objectives. We assess whether we have achieved what we intended and what is the impact on our business by employing such methods as focus groups and follow up surveys.

As part of our evaluation process, we identify specific characteristics that relate to a position and embed them into our hiring practices. Given that our interviews are behavioral-based, we certify that all our assessors are thoroughly trained. We try to look at the employee's potential through the lens of a potential client—does the individual portray the brand we are projecting? We conduct a great deal of best-practices research. We intentionally study companies that do not resemble our own to spur innovation.

BRISTOL MYERS SQUIBB COMPANY

Like most organizations, we are always concerned with having enough talent in the organizational pipeline and supporting people who are already in senior roles. Succession management is an important topic for us. Ours is a dramatically changing environment—we continually have to be aware of developing a deeper bench strength of people with the right skills. We are increasing the rigor of the selection process for those moving into senior roles. We try to use an appropriate balance of promoting from within and making external appointments.

Our organizational culture is very relationship-oriented. We rely on the ability of our individuals to collaborate across the organization to work in a matrix where you lead individuals who do not report to you. To help leaders to understand the broad range of issues confronting senior management, our company holds "senior leadership forums" 8 to 10 times a year with groups of approximately 30 to 35 individuals led by the chairman.

Measurement is always a key issue. We're trying to simplify our assessment process. We are shifting away from a focus only on competency models and beginning to use an approach labeled *business impact interviewing*. Traditionally, in a competency-based system, one starts by translating what we need to have done into a series of competencies, then we assess candidates based on the competencies, and then we translate the competency assessments back into an assessment of whether the candidate can do what we need to have done in the future. With our new approach, we simply ask them if they have done something in the past that is similar to what we need to have done and how they did it, and then we make a judgment whether they can do what we need done in the future.

BOOZ ALLEN HAMILTON

We have established a new leadership initiative, the Fellows Program, that follows an apprentice model. It was driven by our desire to create a standardized leadership development program for our young leaders based around core leadership skills. At the inception stage of this process, senior thought leaders in the organization identified and addressed several critical components:

- To compile a list of the leadership development qualities the organization is looking for in emerging leaders

- To formalize the selection and assessment criteria for those candidates who demonstrate those qualities

- To create a framework of the core activities and projects in which emerging leaders must participate to prepare them for leadership positions in the firm

The Fellow Programs, which is part of our diversity agenda, is global in its focus. It provides a means to identify, in a standardized way, how our young talent can move from organizational manager to organizational leader.

THE VANGUARD GROUP

The challenge is to find the right people who share your values and drive. We strive to fill our leadership pipeline with people who demonstrate a set of traits that we see as nonnegotiable and that form the basis of good business: hard work, ethics, values, and respect at every level. We want people who are intellectual, team players. We look for a diverse pipeline as well, which includes perhaps a different education, upbringing, or career background. We encourage individuality—we don't want cookie-cutter clones. But if the person uses "I" too often, it's a short interview.

You can't pressure individuals to develop and grow into leadership roles faster than their capabilities dictate, but our leaders must, themselves, reflect on how many people they help to develop—as mentors, coaches, and sponsors—and determine what impact they have personally made in advancing leadership development in the firm. We look for people who have the capacity to develop others.

Another important focus for us is creating a strong pool of widely diverse role models. The workforce is changing. Our leadership team is highly representative of the population, but we are always raising the issue, "Are we doing enough to bring along the diverse population within the organization?" Our leadership development takes place over a 10-year time horizon—you have to anticipate environmental changes.

KPMG LLP

Three strategic goals form the underpinning of the vision set out by our chairman and CEO, Eugene D. O'Kelly: to continuously enhance quality through improving our risk architecture and further rebuilding professional credibility, to become the employer of choice by accelerating people development to meet marketplace demands, and to grow profitably, consistent with our quality and human resources initiatives.

Among the initiatives used to accelerate the development of leadership capabilities and careers paths for KPMG LLP's leadership talent are the Chairman's 25 (C25) and the Vice Chairman's 50. The C25 is an accelerated two-year leadership development program for early-career partners, whereas the Vice Chairman's 50 is a leadership development program for emerging leaders and rising stars who are not yet partners.

The KPMG senior leadership has identified the requisite opportunities and commitment for a successful firm partner and has incorporated them into a long-term development process that will become ingrained in the firm's culture over time. In addition to a demonstrated track record of sustained, outstanding performance, C25 candidates are selected based on such skills as change champion, boardroom presence, international experience, and strong people skills.

Our success is measured by how individuals perform when they are able to apply what they've learned in real-world settings. We consider the C25 a success if, at the end of the two-year program, participants affirm that they have, among other activities, provided the chairman and CEO with new and unexpected ideas, identified strategic resources to the firm's success, and formulated strategies, breakthroughs, or novel ideas that can be implemented successfully to make the firm better. In addition, these leaders demonstrate the potential to take on the next critical assignment to support the leadership pipeline and the ability to themselves identify, develop, and lead talent.

In addition to assessing their own perceived success in the initiative, each C25 partner develops a career blueprint for personal and professional growth that is monitored quarterly with their performance managers and is updated continuously for achieving short- and long-term goals. Upward feedback is also used periodically to measure each C25 partner's progress in becoming a better leader. It is important that each C25 partner's leadership development progress is measured and that they are held "accountable" for achieving their desired outcomes.

KPMG employs its "Five Essential Elements of the C25 Curriculum/Experience" to accomplish these objectives. They include a thorough understanding of the firm, skill and competency development, outside learning and thought leadership, development of a comprehensive and cohesive network of C25 colleagues, and proactively taking on the dual roles of mentor and protégé as part of KPMG's mentoring culture. We believe that C25 owes its success in large part to the relevance, shared vision, and commitment of both the individual and the firm.

GOLDMAN SACHS & CO.

Our industry is a very challenging one. Financial services, especially investment banking, is different from other industries. Management *skills* by themselves are somewhat less valued here than in other industries. We look at an individual's commercial *potential* first. Competencies are the second thing we look at. We recognize the value of development. We also see the growing global environment as a challenge: How do we develop local leadership while retaining our culture as an American bank?

We do all the usual components of leadership development—360-degree feedback, rotations, mentoring, and so forth. However, we still follow a strong apprenticeship model—we were a partnership until recently. But now we have nearly 20,000 people instead of 5,000. Our traditional model is difficult to scale up. However, we have created a number of leadership initiatives that include a focus on an evolution in the breadth of leadership responsibility from the self-leader to the new leader through senior management.

With the Leadership/Management Curriculum Program, we are trying to create a consistent common language around leadership from entry level to the highest level. We believe that regardless of context, good leaders do three things very well—they set direction, mobilize commitment, and build capability. Each of our leadership programs teaches these three things at varying levels of complexity.

The Leadership Acceleration Initiative is a one-year program that includes stretch assignments and projects, executive coaching and mentoring, and formal training at two levels: managing directors and select high-performing vice presidents.

Managing directors are prepared for greater and broader leadership responsibility. Teams of senior leaders work together to explore key business issues and opportunities and to learn by doing rather than in the classroom. In addition, relationship building is facilitated among the participants, as well as between participants and the firm's senior leadership. Sponsors guide, coach, and support participants, who are invited to small group "business leader discussions" with senior leaders of the firm.

At the emerging-leader level, there is a focus on relationship building in the group, as well as on increased exposure of participants to senior leadership. Individuals gain a broader perspective of the firm by taking on stretch assignments, as well as enjoying an opportunity to expand their network. Action planning and development review are key elements. Participants are invited to attend speaker series and think tank sessions with senior leaders of the firm, as well as a two-day global workshop. A focus on retaining the most critical talent is demonstrated by investment in the future of this group.

We take the 70/20/10 approach (70 percent of the development is on the job, 20 percent on mentoring/coaching, and 10 percent on training). We take people out of their old area of expertise—we want them to envision what the organization should do strategically using a real-world approach. We've been doing this for about 2 years with extremely positive feedback.

We encourage critical experiences, including managing on a global level and living outside your own region. We have had success using co-headships, a developmental environment in which we team a more experienced person with less experienced one aimed at combining strengths and counteracting weaknesses. The team approach enables more leadership opportunities, as well as the ability to share huge amounts of work. Likewise, it helps in succession, creating a more seamless transition.

We also regularly learn collaboratively with clients through joint programs and initiatives and have been inviting our valued clients to our training programs for the last three years. We find this extremely rewarding because we get fresh perspectives from them and avoid the risk of becoming too inward-looking.

UNISYS

One of our focuses is on building our pipeline. By creating and implementing a comprehensive, benchmark-based plan, we concentrate continuously on developing leaders and potential leaders by giving them greater levels of responsibility, providing blended learning approaches, and always thinking about how we can deliver "just in time" leadership development experiences at the moment when our leaders need them.

We are also focused on providing leaders and future leaders with the proper support as they transition into new roles—from peer to manager— and as they cross over into new geographic, functional, and divisional responsibilities.

Constant feedback and coaching are key in the development of a strong, feedback-based culture. We're encouraging our senior people to get more feedback from colleagues, subordinates, clients, and bosses on an ongoing basis. Since giving feedback is difficult for people, we encourage our leaders to ask their subordinates, "What two things could I be doing differently?" It can take courage to ask this question, but it's very revealing.

Understanding that adults learn and develop in different ways, we blend practical applications with classroom learning. We do segment the audience for some strategies. For example, we have a Career Fitness Center— everyone can use it, but there are specific developmental resources for leaders and potential leaders. In addition, we offer Myers-Briggs assessments, 360-degree evaluations, and strategic development planning and have a thorough annual talent review process.

Building on the success of our Executive Development Forum, an executive network is our next step—we'll be launching it hopefully in the upcoming year. It will concentrate on how high-level executives can build relationships. We want to develop a more virtual and agile environment in which our people can chat and collaborate informally online to solve problems, share ideas, and build stronger social connections.

Everything we do reinforces our plan for leadership. The trend is toward more collaboration, more teaming—we want to build new "legends" of great leaders being successful. We're hiring to this standard. We're starting to see that when individual behavior doesn't match our goals, tough decisions are being made quickly.

MERCK AND CO., INC.

Our company develops leaders around three aspects of leadership excellence: (a) strategic excellence—can people see what needs to be done? (b) execution excellence—can they get it done? and (c) values excellence—can they get it done the right way and in a way that is consistent with our organizational values and ethics?

Our organization is a designed primarily around functions—marketing, finance, research and development (R&D), and so forth. There aren't many opportunities for a general manager's role. We provide broad-based leadership experiences as a substitute in several ways. In classroom programs, we emphasize enterprise-wide issues and focus on the interface across functions, required collaboration, and how to integrate to deal with the complexities of the marketplace. We use simulations to give participants the opportunity to experience how all the issues in the organization interact and to make decisions built on a broader perspective.

We also form worldwide strategic business teams that are built around a particular organizational franchise, such as the cardiovascular unit. The heads of each of the key functional areas in that franchise work together in a team to plan a three- to five-year strategy for that group. They collectively have an opportunity to run that part of the business from a company-wide perspective rather than in a functional capacity. These teams are measured both on performance results and on how they function as a team. We strive to ensure that there is a good cross section in the teams' diversity and representation.

To develop future leaders, we identify what new competencies we will need 5 to 10 years in the future. For example, we will need leaders who can work in alliances with academia and with other companies—even those who traditionally may have been our competitors—as well as with strategic partners in biotech and other fields. Future leaders will have to learn how to cross over traditional boundaries, working in virtual organizations. They must learn how to make decisions and reach agreement in these new environments.

We also will need leaders who can confront a more competitive environment by developing a greater risk tolerance. This never means risking patient safety. Rather, it means the ability to execute by balancing the rigor of assessment with agility.

Our company conducts an annual formal human resources planning assessment that is reviewed by our CEO. We take an inventory of the progress we've made on leadership development. We look at key strategies and ask ourselves if we have made enough progress toward meeting our goals—are there high enough levels of diversity and country representation? Is our pipeline sufficiently robust? We take a holistic view of our initiatives to ensure that we have the talent needed to succeed.

THE JUDGE INSTITUTE OF MANAGEMENT, UNIVERSITY OF CAMBRIDGE

The future is highly uncertain and complex. We want to teach capabilities that are sustainable over the next 20 or more years. There is a core framework of leadership fundamentals and values. We want to embed these elements so that they are readily accessible in the midst of the everyday decision-making process. Part of this is also to focus on motivating and enabling others around a vision, as well as setting stretch targets and managing and evaluating performance.

We promote a profound understanding of leadership in yourself and in others. We emphasize the need to balance various roles that may be filled by oneself or others—for example: figurehead, spokesperson, and motivator—the embodiment of core values, and the importance of always paying attention to each role as part of a greater network of relationships. Whenever you really analyze great examples of leadership, it is rare in contemporary business or culture for there to be a single hero or heroine. Future leaders must learn not only to value others but also to see and bring out the best that comes from a celebration of diversity. They must cross boundaries by taking an interdisciplinary and global view. This is especially important given the global search for talent and creativity and the discerning aspirations of those on whom future achievements in business, politics, and community development will depend.

We stress an understanding of a wider context—the global economy, geopolitics, competition for natural resources, rising public expectations for participation and power in decisions that have profound effects on daily life across the globe, and international regulation, as well as competition. This does not underestimate the vital importance of competitive business decisions and actions but looks to create future generations of leaders who are realistically committed to building sustainable organizations that will yield clearly recognized benefits for their stakeholders. For commercial organizations, this means securing the basis for building long-term shareholder value.

As a business school, we are concerned not only with advancing leadership through our teaching and learning but also with advancing knowledge through rigorous and relevant research. We take a collaborative approach to sharing knowledge and conducting research. We have created and continue to create partnerships with the world of practice, with corporations, and with not-for-profit organizations, as well as collaboratively with other business schools.

SPRINT

One of our goals is to find the right development experience for each individual and the right amount of support throughout the learning process. Successful learning is a combination of the right person, at the right time, in the right assignment. Our approach is to give appropriate stretch assignments that challenge the individuals in the targeted leadership program in new ways: turnarounds, large team assignments, newly formed teams, and so forth. We give these emerging leaders a safety net but also the ability to learn. We encourage our people to stretch outside their comfort zones, but we try to apply the right balance of providing support without micromanaging them.

We use a robust performance feedback approach. It is a highly interactive and collaborative experience. At set intervals we bring together the employees' current and former rotation managers and bosses for a comprehensive, systematic evaluation discussion that covers five leadership dimensions. People are assessed against these leadership dimensions, as well as against other individuals in similar situations, at similar levels, in the organization. The notes from this meeting are sent to the attendees for approval and any necessary modification and, following that, are sent to the employee for review. A follow-up meeting is scheduled with the employee, the development program manager, and the current rotation manager to ensure that the employee has an opportunity for additional clarification and that the subsequent development plans incorporate the panel feedback.

We address where individuals are doing well but also where they need additional development and more opportunities to round out their career experience. Individuals work with their managers to explore future directions—do they need experience leading a larger team? Responsibility for financial deliverables? A specific mix of functional experience?

The evaluation also involves a reflective component—individuals respond to the question, "If this person were promoted, what is the one thing that could cause him or her to fail?" In addition, managers also determine what elements emerging leaders will need for their next rotation and what resources the company must provide. As a result of the process, the individual takes away a comprehensive written document that is a past-focused and future-focused leadership development plan.

ALLSTATE INSURANCE CO.

As part of the leadership development process, we are continually aligning, integrating, and reinforcing HR processes that have an impact on the flow of talent. As part of the process, we strive to understand what the market imperatives are, what our organizational imperatives are, and assess what our people in key roles will need. As strategies change, we revisit our list of key competencies to ensure that they meet our projected business needs over the next three to five years.

We are very aggressive about identifying and developing those capabilities people must demonstrate to better meet our strategic agenda. For example, one aspect of our strategy is to be very customer-centric; therefore, one component of our approach to development must be from the frame of reference of a customer focus and customer experience. We define what leaders must do to better meet customer needs. In addition, we look for those who exhibit behaviors that are driving change around customer needs in our business. Similarly, as growth or operational efficiency increasingly becomes a strategic issue for us in the future, we are consistently screening and selecting for those who have growth or operational efficiency backgrounds and outlooks.

Our journey over the next three to four years will focus on HR processes and people decision systems. We will ask the questions about how performance management, coaching, education, selection, and succession management all connect. We are finding ways to better enable HR processes to support and drive business priorities. We also want to increase our focus on team-oriented performance rewards.

COLGATE-PALMOLIVE

There is an extremely global context in our organization. However, the majority of other companies are intensely interested in the same people for the significant operating jobs. Everyone understands the need to be more creative in the way they approach this challenge. We look at the world as a whole, not only as regions. There is a shrinking pool of talent—or just not enough talent, specifically people with global perspective. We model a global view into everything we do—it's how our business is run—in each P&L center, in thinking about decisions and staffing, and so forth. There is an ongoing process to calibrate: "Is the bench strength there?" If not, recalibrate. Our culture is, "Always look at diversity on a global basis; look at the feeder pools."

There is a commitment to global leadership development. It is not HR-driven; it is driven by function heads and other line leaders. Likewise, although training and executive education are important, on-the-job experiences are the key. Succession planning is line-driven. The tools, processes, and approaches are consistent everywhere in the world. And in every development session there are general managers, division vice presidents, and other senior executives involved in the process. There is commitment from senior management—top people are interested in being involved.

We have created and use global tools: succession planning, two Web-based 360-degree assessments, and coaching. In "Colgate Leaders Teach," the goal is that all high potentials teach at least one course. They get outstanding exposure to more senior leaders. Through our "train the trainers" approach to global training, participants may be trained in the United States, for example, but may have to go to Latin America or Europe to conduct programs. We use this approach for leadership and functional training. In the program development phase, we work with key people from each of four operating divisions to run focus groups, test applicability of course content, and find out such things as, "Does the information translate well into Chinese?" They know the questions to ask.

We don't have 300 different programs—we have a number of good, consistent ones. We have found that our programs "just make sense." It is about simplicity—we ask, "How is our division manager going to understand it, use it?" We want to be able to say, "Here are the five basic things we need to be consistent." We focus on the simple and practical. This allows for local adaptation while setting global minimum standards for development.

DELOITTE & TOUCHE USA LLP

A critical competency for our high potentials is the ability to communicate with their teams to get the best from them—to communicate a clear vision. We monitor our emerging leaders as we give them increasingly greater opportunities to make sure that their communication skills remain commensurate with their growing responsibilities.

We identify our several hundred top leaders—those who are currently in those roles or will be there in the next three to four years. This group receives specialized leadership development—programs that have been created through partnerships with business schools worldwide.

Leadership development is driven from the top down by our senior leadership steering committee—they determine what skills sets, deployments, and committees will be necessary for each of the top roles from a succession-planning perspective.

JPMORGANCHASE

In revenue-generating lines of business, taking promising leaders off the job to develop them is a challenge. Therefore, we encourage managers to integrate actual business experiences into the leadership development process—to be thoughtful about selecting appropriate roles, projects, client interactions, and so forth that will enhance their team members' development rather than simply assigning them tasks that accompany a specific position.

It is also important for us to apply a high degree of rigor and discipline in creating our talent review processes—to ask the right questions and to reflect on the approach in order to quantify the quality of our development initiatives. It requires that leaders integrate human capital management into the overall business planning process. The leadership development process is becoming more fact-based rather than intuitive.

✧

The following organizations have chosen to remain anonymous. Their insights, however, provide an additional wealth of knowledge on the latest trends in leadership initiatives.

We are focused on the development of talent, the development of others, as well as yourself, coaching others, and providing feedback. We are looking at both near-term and long-term performance, with a commitment to developing a culture of inclusivity and diversity, unleashing the best thinking, the best effort of all people. How do you do this? The three C's: *change, coaching,* and *culture.*

We're looking at long-term sustainability. Vice presidents, division presidents, and other experienced leaders develop new leaders to sustain organizational leadership for the long term by focusing on discipline, rigor, and continuity. Our environment demands strong, well-rounded overall leaders that have physical and emotional stamina for the long run. Leadership development is an enterprise-wide asset—not one that is housed in business development only. We collaboratively assess workplace capability needs, recruitment and pipeline issues, and what we need to do to facilitate our internal and external growth. We also focus on all our assets—not just sales talent or specific functional areas—but broad-based leadership experience. Our strategy is to focus on an enterprise-wide full life cycle that includes selection criteria to meet our current needs and future competencies and deployment of human assets.

✧

Our profession is faced with great complexity and new challenges, the most profound of which is a new regulatory approach and focus in both our U.S. and worldwide markets. This has changed the way we do business significantly. Change management is a critical issue. We have to change the paradigm of how we do business. In response, we are increasing learning opportunities within the firm.

Our business environment is also becoming more global. Many of our future leaders will need expertise outside their home countries and will require an openness to thinking in a more global mind-set.

To proactively address this reality, we created a senior-level committee to focus on a global learning strategy. At its inception, members from eight different countries participated in global debates to resolve the organization's strategic issues.

Leadership development in our firm is a collaborative, rather than individual, undertaking. There are tremendous opportunities to learn not only from the senior managers but also from the younger leaders as well. We also look beyond our own company to build relationships with outside experts. For example, we have created an advisory board with academic leaders, who engage us in exciting debates. With their help, we have designed new learning programs, such as a more comprehensive executive development system.

∽

As a result of growth and acquisitions that have created a truly global firm, our organization now has incorporated numerous leaders, styles, and cultures. We have adopted a new mission statement and a set of core values in which each business maintains its own personality but fits within a single organizational culture.

Based on leadership standards established and articulated by our CEO, we have introduced a number of initiatives. Among them is a six- to nine-month action learning program for senior leaders. General management issues are posed in the program and drive the leadership agenda—participants respond to our critical business challenges.

We address talent development by first asking who we are targeting, and then what do we do with them? Whether for first-line managers or senior management, development options are based around leadership and on accountabilities. These include highly tailored shorter-duration options: executive coaching, interview- and Web-based 360-degree assessments, internal and external leadership programs, stretch assignments, and a suite of psychometric exercises.

We identify talent and develop tailored offerings to those individuals from a portfolio of development options. One critical feature is that they are always leader-led and aimed at building the culture. We believe that leadership development should be done by the leaders themselves. The role of HR is to facilitate the process. If we have a group of assistant vice presidents, we bring in a managing director to facilitate and to work with them. It works fantastically well. It sends a message and says a lot about the next generation of senior leaders, helping out in the development process. Our leadership development is tied to strategy. Although the connotation of the word *potential* in assessing future leadership success can vary from business to business, all initiatives are based around performance and results.

☙

We are focused on getting our stakeholders aligned and engaged in consistent leadership development.

Our strategy is that development occurs on the job: providing the best coaching support and recognizing that opportunities for learning and development frequently occur at key transition points in individuals' careers. We send people to classes but find that most of the development occurs afterward. Leadership development involves about 70 percent on-the-job experience, 20 percent coaching, and 10 percent learning activities. We include formal learning experiences, depending on the level of the leader, that target transitions to leader roles. First-line leaders receive a toolkit of readings and resources that is self-paced and self-guided, not programmatic. It focuses on what to expect and on building skills for the transition experience.

Midlevel leaders supervising first-level managers are given the chance to go to transition programs. For three and a half days they work on the role transition of managing at a higher level and on accelerating their transition through work planning, skill building, leading larger departments, and understanding the situation and nature of what they'll be doing, such as leading a turnaround or startup.

At the executive level, we include small teams that deal with knowledge transfer. We address knowledge process and strategy—capturing what the executive tacitly knows (the informal pieces of what they do). A number of people are involved. We look at "unconscious competence"—you can't articulate it; it's the many forms of information and knowledge that they have acquired over years.

We have an integrated, graduated curriculum strategy for leaders. It addresses what leaders need at each successive level and builds on the previous foundations of leadership learning. In addition, we have many cross-functional teams. We are also beginning to include rotations, internships, and short assignments that involve participating in a related role doing different work—individuals are immersed in a project for someone else.

☙

Within certain of our business units that have become major growth areas, our challenges include not just attention to developing our people but also attention to the speed with which we can do it. We take a longer-term view and make it part of our people-focused, leadership-focused culture.

We have begun to address the leadership development needs of our midlevel managers. Our organization is highly decentralized, so remote learning and online learning are very important. One challenge is meeting the needs of our employees who are less technology/Internet-friendly. Another challenge to this approach in more remote locations is the limitation of bandwidth. We want to do more streaming video—more interactive opportunities that the increased speed of technology can enable.

Development strategies include a one-year program designed to build strategic leadership skills that prepares senior managers for executive roles. This initiative includes a 360-degree assessment component, executive coaching, a two-week mini-MBA course, and an experiential leadership development component in the wilderness. At the end of the program, participants present recommendations pertaining to the strategic business issues of senior management.

We also have initiated an e-learning leadership development piece that is integrated into performance management and succession planning. It assesses and develops an array of essential leadership competencies, including trust building and respect, effective communication, conflict resolution, customer focus, and the inspiration of others. It is a self-driven process that includes assessments, development process plans, feedback, and tracking. Participants review their development plans with their managers, including goals, a time frame, and opportunities for feedback and coaching. Surveys examine feedback, learning that took place, changes in behavior, and other important elements of reflective leadership learning.

☙

Our strategy acknowledges that we can't provide equal attention to all our leaders at the same time. We therefore concentrate a significant portion of our development resources on our top 10 percent. This includes coaching, executive- and 360-degree-based assessments, on-the-job learning (rotations, performance consultancy), real-time learning initiatives and action reviews, real-world experience, cross-company town meetings, and debriefings.

We customize interventions and then augment them with enterprise-specific learning opportunities that bring leaders together to discuss and address specific business challenges. We apply a top-management perspective at the business-specific level. Human resources executives also partner with local academic institutions to work on specific business challenges (e.g., focusing on breaking into new markets, best practices, and planning). We work with professors, thought leaders, and others.

Anecdotally, some of our more popular programs seem to include short-term solutions-focused programs featuring an expert resource (a "name"). However, most leaders are astute enough to appreciate that the personal touch is best in the long term. They want to know, "What can I do differently today to address tomorrow's challenges?"

cℳ

In assessing talent, we want to make sure that emerging leaders have the capacity to grow. As part of the succession planning process, we conduct many in-depth interviews and organize yearly talent assessments to uncover what leaders can do. These sessions are a focused review where leadership teams look at a variety of areas: leadership and talent assessment, organizational structure, management succession, key training and development plans, and strategic business imperatives.

Part of an individual's leadership development comes from being stretched by taking on a participative role. People often learn best through specific experiences, in addition to feedback and coaching—drawing on lessons learned and reflecting on them in terms of what they learned. It's not enough just to take action; it is critical to reflect on that action as well. It is important to expose emerging leaders to opportunities—in off-site sessions, for example, they can interact with other leaders and gain greater knowledge of industry issues. We also have introduced a peer-coaching model—a one-week program with feedback and coaches aimed at refining one's own leadership development.

In conducting executive assessments, we hold extended interviews with our candidates, looking for themes and insights into their interests and life transitions. The participants also provide a wide range of references from among their peers, subordinates, customers, bosses, and others. These conversations provide a broader perspective on the major themes in the candidate's makeup.

∽

First, we are interested in identifying leaders in the company who can address our current and future business problems. Second, we get people to think increasingly about intangibles—not only past performance of our future leaders, but their potential for the future business issues and their ability to learn—how well they have done on projects and assignments. We then work to tie this to the selection process.

When we interview candidates, we frequently just sit down and talk as part of the process. We often identify the people who can learn in a non-threatening way. Past examples of how they learn can give us an indication of future learning capability. In addition to the interview, we also gain valuable insights and information from the sponsor—the person who's putting the individual forward as a high potential. We create an experience map—a way of comparing our people across the organization through their experiences—in an effort to compare apples and apples. Have these people had the same sort of experiences? Have they been involved or led a turnaround or a startup? Did they experience a staff-to-line switch, and how did they survive it? How have they succeeded? It elevates the discussion. We give high potentials a range of experiences, such as domestic and international rotations.

All our leadership programs include a consistent message: "You have to learn."

∽

One challenge we face is time off the job, which can be significant, owing to many demands to balance. We perform on-the-job development well and must leverage on-the-job learning and experience. We encourage both managers and participants to think of development beyond individual training programs and more in terms of on-the-job projects and work assignments. Managers should be pointing out and giving thought to how projects and client activity lead to development—making connections about goals and objectives and identifying how these actions will be a part of their team members' development.

We structure development for jobs in similar categories to facilitate more effective leadership development in certain areas. We can say, "These are the fundamental skills and competencies for this particular position at this level."

At various stages moving toward a given job category, we can determine what you start with in a particular stage, monitor progress against developmental skill outcomes for that stage, and determine whether or not effective progress has been demonstrated. Over time it becomes more and more clear to both the employee and the manager what certain competencies should look like when they are being demonstrated effectively. It becomes less about the training program and more about what the employee did with the learning after coming back on the job and applying that learning. Managers observe and validate the process. People don't move to the next phase until we see evident, noticeable, and consistent developmental progress at that level—it usually takes a couple of years. A person could be a sales rep in one business unit and then become a manager in another business unit because the process and the skills targeted for management development are the same.

However, it's more difficult in noncomparable job categories. Here we define standards required at a certain level versus defining the exact skills needed in a specific job. Examples could include how well the individual contributes, what her people skills look like, how she leads on strategic issues, and so forth. We then look at each level and come up with a standardized definition of what success encompasses. Applying those defined characteristics by level in a well-defined succession-planning process enables identification of a pipeline of talent through the organization. The succession-planning process is conducted in facilitated meetings to maintain consistency and fairness. Essentially no one manager can assess his own direct reports in a vacuum. They will be challenged during the meeting by their peers using the agreed-on criteria and characteristics.

We have identified critical leadership positions and what the necessary characteristics and competencies are for those positions. By tracking the talent pipeline at different stages—current, near term, and long term—we quickly get a sense of possible gaps. We also can look at other characteristics of our pipeline, such as experience in a global setting and in a startup or turnaround situation, as well as the diversity mix, cross-functional experience, and any other pertinent competencies or characteristics needed in our talent pipeline over time.

Each year we conduct a succession-planning audit to see if the prior-year development plans have resulted in developmental progress, and if they have not, we investigate possible reasons. In addition to providing data about the robustness of our talent pipeline, this annual review drives accountability with managers to stay committed to the development plans for their employees.

We not only work to define competencies needed at different levels of the organization and to execute a succession-planning process to assess the talent pipeline, but we also look at leadership development support during the critical transition points—at first-time supervisors of peers or in new roles, such as starting a new business.

We have started to look at several major areas for leadership development: The first looks at what changes are needed to move to the next level: a track record of managing conflict and taking risks to deal with change, for example. The second area examines the ability of an individual with a solid track record to learn quickly and produce results in a new role. The third element involves their ability to collaborate and to get results by delegating, influencing, building trust, building and rebuilding confidence, and motivating others. To assess this capability, we observe individuals in relationships across departments and functions and in interactions with peers, as well as through feedback from colleagues and team members.

cらか

How to measure our effectiveness is an area of particular focus for us. One of our goals is to identify and implement a common model for understanding the issues for all leaders—first level, midlevel, and executive level. One aspect of this model is creating a feedback mechanism that can be used consistently across the organization to reinforce an organizational culture for giving and getting feedback.

We have a detailed process for promotions. For more senior levels, we hold "peer interviews," in which each business line's candidates for promotion are presented and reviewed by managing directors in other areas of the business. Candidates are evaluated on the "3 P's": platforms (the job they're in), performance, and personal impact. The third element is the most difficult to quantify but involves the degree to which the candidate makes contributions to the firm, acts as a role model or "culture carrier," and becomes actively involved in the internal and external activities of the business.

cらか

Our leadership development initiatives take a two-pronged approach to meeting current and future organizational leadership needs. First, we want to develop inspirational leaders. These are leaders who can identify and articulate why they are in their roles in our organization and in our industry. They are able, even more importantly, to communicate this purpose to others. This coherent, shared vision motivates their team members and peers to grow and develop further.

The other critical aim of our leadership development initiatives is to foster excellence in execution—operational excellence, streamlining processes, and so forth.

To better meet these current and future needs, we are introducing a leadership model that focuses on developing several critical competencies: high-performance behaviors that enable leaders to collaborate and make sense of today's and tomorrow's environments, knowledge management, concept formation, and empathetic leadership styles.

Since these new capabilities are often challenging to assess, we rely on development centers and work shadowing, where internal and external experts observe and evaluate emerging leaders in their work settings.

cᴧɔ

Augmenting bench strength has become a major issue and strategic goal for our industry. We are now embarking on a new course of action that involves developing people on three levels. Our first group of interest consists of very senior people who constitute the most critical positions across the enterprise. Senior management is involved in identifying and working with these top people in the areas of recruiting and succession planning.

The second group includes the next generation of leaders. These very high potentials are the ones that all organizations want. We give them opportunities to contribute and to assume major roles in startups and key projects. We project that in three to five years they will move into our top leadership group.

The third group encompasses the emerging leaders—the long-term future of the company, 10 years or so in the future. They are currently going into enterprise-wide businesses and functions. We create exposure for them to emerge as outstanding individuals. One keen focus at this level is diversity. We want to track where members of this group go as they transition from this level to the next. We also want to verify that there is a consistent level of diverse representation throughout.

We are looking at strategy beyond the short term. This involves taking talent management to a global level.

Endnotes

Introduction: The New Epic Leader
1. Ann Barrett and John Beeson, *Developing Leaders for 2010,* New York: The Conference Board, 2002, p. 3.
2. Ibid.
3. www.mckinseyquarterly.com.
4. Michael Wonacott, "Gold Collar Workers," *ERIC Digest,* 2002, report no. EDO-CE-02-234.
5. www.susandunn.cc/index.htm.
6. www.mckinseyquarterly.com.

Success Secret #1: Cross-Functional/Interdisciplinary Thinking: Having the Knowledge and Using It
1. Michael Wonacott, "Gold Collar Workers," *ERIC Digest,* 2002, report no. EDO-CE-02-234.
2. Stratford Sherman, "How Tomorrow's Leaders Are Learning Their Stuff," *Fortune,* November 27, 1995, p. 93.
3. Nicholas H. Farnham, "Empowering Leaders to Speak Out for Liberal Education," *Liberal Education Online,* Summer 2003.

Success Secret #2: Maximizing Your Leadership: Leading with Passion, Energy, and Emotional Intelligence
1. Stephen Green, Fred Hassan, Jeffrey Immelt, Michael Marks, and Daniel Meiland, "In Search of Global Leaders," *Harvard Business Review,* August 2003, pp. 40–41.
2. Daniel Goleman, *Emotional Intelligence,* New York: Bantam Books, 1995.

Success Secret #3: Managing Your Knowledge Networks
1. www.pwc.global.com.
2. Charnell Havens and Ellen Knapp, "Easing into Knowledge Management," *Strategy and Leadership*, March–April 1999, p. 8.
3. "Staying Afloat and Staying Ahead," *Knowledge Management*, June 2002, pp. 18–19.
4. Charnell Havens and Ellen Knapp, "Easing into Knowledge Management," *Strategy and Leadership*, March–April 1999, p. 8.

Success Secret #5: Creating a Culture of Integrity and Values
1. Ian Wilson, "The New Rules," *Strategy and Leadership* 28(3), 2000, p. 15.
2. Jessi Hempel and Lauren Gard, "Special Report—Philanthropy 2004, The Corporate Givers," *Business Week Online*, November 29, 2004.
3. Ibid.
4. Stratford Sherman, "How Tomorrow's Leaders Are Learning Their Stuff," *Fortune*, November 27, 1995, p. 93.

Success Secret #6: Leading in a Diverse Environment
1. David Thomas, "The Truth About Mentoring Minorities: Race Matters," *Harvard Business Review*, April 2000, p. 103.
2. Blackenterprise.com.

Success Secret #7: Developing a Mentoring Network
1. David Thomas, "The Truth About Mentoring Minorities: Race Matters," *Harvard Business Review*, April 2000, p. 103.

Success Secret #8: Expanding Your Global Focus
1. Linda Hill, "Collective Genius," *Executive Excellence*, December 2000, p. 17.
2. Stephen Green, Fred Hassan, Jeffrey Immelt, Michael Marks, and Daniel Meiland, "In Search of Global Leaders," *Harvard Business Review*, August 2003, pp. 40–41.
3. Ibid.
4. Linda Hill, "Collective Genius," *Executive Excellence*, December 2000, p. 17.
5. Richard Florida, "America's Looming Creativity Crisis," *Harvard Business Review*, October 2004, p. 124.
6. Ibid.

7. Richard Florida, "America's Looming Creativity Crisis," *Harvard Business Review*, October 2004, p. 124.
8. Linda Hill, "Collective Genius," *Executive Excellence*, December 2000, p. 17.
9. www.net-magic.net/worldhomes.
10. Linda Hill, "Collective Genius," *Executive Excellence*, December 2000, p. 17.
11. Rosabeth Moss Kanter. "Change Is Everyone's Job: Managing the Extended Enterprise in a Globally Connected World," *Organizational Dynamics*, Summer 1999, p. 13.

Success Secret #9:   Building and Leading High-Performance Teams
1. Linda Hill, "Collective Genius," *Executive Excellence*, December 2000, p. 17.
2. Gary Klein, "Why Won't They Follow Simple Directions?" *Across the Board*, February 2000, p. 18.

Success Secret #10:   Leading—and Thriving—in an Environment of Ambiguity, Uncertainty, and Change
1. Randall P. White and Philip Hodgson, "Leadership? The Ne(x)t Generation," *Directions—The Ashridge Journal*, Summer 2001, p. 18.
2. Paul Shoemaker and Franck Schuurmans, "Opportunity Is Uncertainty," *Association Management*, December 2003, p. 50.

Index

Volatility:
    preparing for, 122–126
    in VUCA (volatility, uncertainty,
        complexity, ambiguity) model,
        115–127
Volunteer work, 54–55
VUCA (volatility, uncertainty, complex-
    ity, ambiguity) model, 115–127

"War for talent," xvii
Welch, Jack, 19, 109

Women:
    diversity and, 55, 63–69, 80–81
    mentoring relationships and,
        80–81
Work-based learning, 132
World Homes, 90
World Trade Center attacks (2001), 19,
    120–122, 124
Writing skills, 47–49

Xerox, 53

About the Authors

Donna and Lynn Brooks have conducted extensive research into emerging trends and best practices in organizational leadership. For *Ten Secrets of Successful Leaders*, the Brooks twins interviewed leaders and leadership development experts from many of the most highly respected organizations worldwide. Based on their findings, they have created an innovative model, *The New Epic Leader*©, which offers insights into leadership success for aspiring and experienced leaders alike.

In their roles as consultants, speakers, and educators, Donna and Lynn have had the opportunity to share perspectives on leadership with thought leaders in a wide range of fields. In addition, Donna received a doctorate in adult and organizational development, while Lynn's doctoral studies focused on organizational leadership, which reinforced her 15 years' experience in international sales and marketing management. Both Donna and Lynn have lived, worked, and traveled extensively abroad—in Europe, Asia/Pacific, Latin America, and Africa. They both attended universities in France and Italy and speak several languages.

Donna and Lynn have been interviewed by major media outlets worldwide, including CNN, CNBC, the *Wall Street Journal*, *BusinessWeek*, Fast Company, NPR, and many others. The Brooks sisters are also the authors of *Seven Secrets of Successful Women* (McGraw-Hill, 1997) and *Ten Secrets of Successful Men That Women Want to Know* (McGraw-Hill, 2002). For more information, please visit their Web site at www.dlbrooksconsulting.com.